ONCE IN A LIFETIME COMES A MAN

ONCE IN A LIFETIME COMES A MAN

GRACE LARSON

Once In A Lifetime Comes A Man
Copyright © 2021 by Grace Larson.

Parchment Global Publishing
1500 Market Street, 12th Floor, East Tower
Philadelphia, Pennsylvania, 19102
www.parchmentglobalpublishing.com

All rights reserved. No part of this book may be reproduced or transmitted in any form or by any means, electronic or mechanical, including photocopying, recording, or by any information storage and retrieval, system, without permission in writing from the copyright owner.

ISBN: 978-1-952302-86-2 (sc)
ISBN: 978-1-952302-85-5 (e)

Library of Congress Control Number: 2021917551

Contents

Acknowledgements vii
Prologue 1
Reminiscing 3
Family In Photos 12
Lyle's Early Years 22
Navy Sea Bee 25
Time 30
Love At First Sight 32
Destiny 34
Letters 36
Rain And Humor 46
Wisconsin Bound 50
Vacation Is Over 53
Summer Letters 55
Wisconsin Again 62
Back In College 64
More Letters From Lyle 67
Leaving The Farm 77
Spokane 79
Our Song 81
Our Wedding 83
Another Dream 85
Enjoying Spokane 87
Colstrip 90
Putting Down Roots 95
Changes 98
The Big Red Dog 100
Exploring 103
Our New House 113
Back Country Driving 116
More Exploring 118
Aging And Loss 120
Lyle's Life In Pictures 125

More Trips, Family, And Wood	138
Our Love Notes	142
Our Last December	148
Moving On	154
End Photos	157
Epilogue	161
Author Biography	163

ACKNOWLEDGEMENTS

A NCESTRY.COM
City of Spokane and Gary Nance for the Carousal Photo
EMI Christian Music Store and www.capitolcmglicensing.com for allowing me to use "Russ's Song" in this book.

I have used excerpts from Lyle's letters to me in 1982. I have used some of my correspondence to him, but very little, because those letters would equal an encyclopedia. Every time we were apart during the years of our life together, I had sent letters to Lyle. Throughout 1982, and then during our years together whenever we'd be apart; letters sent from Minnesota, Wisconsin, Colorado Springs, and California.

Our letters have filled 2 very large notebooks. Cards expressing our love for each other have filled another large notebook.

This is the story of my husband's life. I only hope I was a Blessing to him as he surely was to me.

PROLOGUE

FATE WAS A blessing when a dream brought Lyle into my life once more. He was 46 years old and had never married. It had been 18 years since we'd seen each other. I was almost 42 with 3 adult children and 2 ready to graduate high school.

It is only once in a lifetime that a person is lucky enough to have true love. I had that with Lyle, and it is only with writing this book and reading his letters that I fully realize the depth of his being and his love for me.

I heard this on a news program on marriage: "It is rewarding to know someone has been a wit-ness to your life." I am that witness to Lyle's life. "Our song will endure through eternity."

I hope that in reading this you will appreciate the soft heart, humor, intelligence, and love that was Lyle. The love he had for his family, animals, and creation. He was a man of integrity and fine character, and a good listener. The mark of a man is how a man lives his life and my husband was that man; a good man who had a great mother and father. "Once In A Lifetime Comes A Man."

REMINISCING

Lyle and his father, Arthur Larson 1937

Lyle's mother, Annie Ebensperger Larson

From ancestry.com:

Name:
Annie Ebensperger
[Annie Ebersberger]
Age: 11
Birth Date Oct 1888
Birthplace: Wisconsin
Home in 1900: Union, Pierce, Wisconsin
Race: White
Gender: Female
Relation to Head of House: Daughter (Child)
Marital Status: Single
Father's name: J Etemsperger
Father's Birthplace: Switzerland
Mother's name: Caroline Etemsperger
Mother's Birthplace: Switzerland

Name: Robert Arthur Larson
Birth Date: 12 Aug 1886
Birth Place: Burnside, Goodhue, Minnesota (Prairie Island)
Gender: Male
Race: White
Father's name: Hans L
Father's Birth Place: Sweden
Mother's name: Annie Suter

Name: Annie Ebensperger
Gender: Female
Marriage Date: 1 Jan 1912
Marriage Place: St Paul, Ramsey, Minnesota
Spouse's Name: Arthur Larson
Spouse Gender: Male
Event Type: Marriage

Deaths:
| Larson | Arthur R. | 1886-1973 - |
| " | Annie E. | 1888-1964 - |

Name: Lyle Vernon Larson
Birth Date: 1 Jan 1936

Birth Place: Salem (Pierce County), Pierce County, Wisconsin, USA
Death Date: 16 Dec 2013
Death Place: Forsyth, Rosebud County, Montana, USA Cemetery: Murray Memorial Cemetery
Burial: Lonepine, Sanders County, Montana, USA

Larson Farm

Notes taken as Lyle talked about his life and family:

My mother and Dad met when Dad was working on a haying crew for a man named Hunn. He met Dad at the 4th of July Celebration in Plum City where they would be haying the next day.

"Would Dad go pick that little Ebensperger girl up?" Mr. Hunn thought she kind of liked Dad. Dad picked her up and took her out to Hunn's. Mother also worked in a hotel in Maiden Rock and hotels in St. Paul. They were married on New Year's Day in St. Paul on 1-1- 1912. More than likely Dad's side of the family attended because quite a few of them lived in St. Paul. I was born on New Year's Day in 1936 on their 24th Wedding Anniversary. I was named after Aunt Caroline's husband, Lyle. My Mother wanted to call me Paul. I think that is probably why I ended up being called Bud; my mother didn't like the name, Lyle.

They didn't live on the farm as soon as they were married. They lived over by Charlie Sticht's farm. One Sunday they went for a drive with the team and went past the farm I grew up on. Mother thought it an absolute dump not realizing she'd be living there.

The size of the farm was 80 acres. Dad borrowed the money to buy it from Julius, his brother. He was able to pay that off quickly, then he borrowed enough from the bank to build the barn. When the Depression came along Dad almost lost the place; "too bad he didn't as he might have found a better place with less rock and better soil."

Dad was born on Prairie Island and Mother was born in a house in Plum City. Mother's father's name was Heinrich (Henry) Ebensperger. I don't know what Mother's mother's name was. Dad couldn't stand her. Mother came from a big family; her and Bertha, several sisters, and 4 brothers. Bertha and Mom were close in age. Her brothers were Jake, John, Henry, and Fred. Henry was born in Switzerland before they were married. He ran away as a teen and was never heard from again. The only one I knew was Fred. He'd come visit his daughter, who was married to a man named Heinzer, who owned the Grange Hall Store. Her name was Carol. Fred owned some apartments in Red Wing. He was a hard drinker as most of the Ebensperger boys were. John married a widow, Mary, who was Catholic. That made her feel bad so she had him converted to Catholic on his death bed. This made Mother very angry! I liked Aunt Mary and stayed with her when I was in high school. They had a son named Henry, named after his uncle and grandfather, who was kind of a hero during WWII. Henry worked at the Grange Hall store. He married a girl, a beautiful divorcee, from the Methodist Church. My sister, Alice said, "well it didn't work with a Methodist so maybe it will work with a Catholic." Henry was Catholic. They had several children that would be middle aged or retired by now.

The Suters which are Dad's family lived around Plum City. So it is possible the Epensbergers and Suters may have married. Dad used to talk about Door Suter. His name was Theodore. Dad's mother was a Suter but she was one of 22 kids. Aunt Mary Martin was her sister.

Mother raised chickens and traded eggs for groceries. Dad called it "trade" all of his life. They sold milk when I was young. They sold cream before that. Cream stayed fresh longer without refrigeration. Dad always farmed with horses. He had 3 horses, 12 cows, and about 50 to 65 sheep; that was all the place would carry.

Dad paid for the place by hauling wood to Lake City. He'd cross the ice with his team and sled going from Maiden Rock to Lake City, MN. Dad would often come home so cold he couldn't do more than get off the wagon. Mother would put the team away so he could go into the house and get warm. Mother did a lot of the milking when Dad was hauling wood, and this was by hand.

Mother made the best bread. A treat was her bread lathered with butter and topped with sugar. I'd have had that in my lunch pail every day if Mother would have sent it. I did go to the ice cream place in Plum City and have a big sundae or some other ice cream treat. My mother gave me enough money for this several times a week. She practically supported the farm with her egg money.

When Bernard and Art were small, they'd come to visit while I was in school, and they'd get into my room and my stuff; some of those stuffs were the cut outs of forts and buildings from cereal boxes. Typical younger boys who were like brothers to me.

When Dad built the garage a big Swede Dad called The Big Swede sawed the lumber. Marlin Volt and I carried the logs. We were both real strong. At meal time I would have to go to the locker at Grange Hall and get some meat; in those days' radiators were always drained; I could have taken Swede's car but he had drained it. (Lyle didn't say if he had to walk or what as his Dad didn't have a car.)

I had never seen a drunk until the Swede and his sawyers had gone fishing; they were drunk and fell in the water, and they kept repeating themselves all the time. The one sawyer, a man named, Hague, was a bachelor. He was really quiet but when his friend, Gus, left to go to the dance, Hague sat and talked to Dad. Their old sawmill was so beat up and the tractor was old. But they could saw the most beautiful wood. When Dad built the sheep shed the sawyer was from Pepin. He had a modern mill. Kenny was a small boy then; he said, "So that's where boards come from."

We usually ran out of propane at meal time so I'd have to go to Maiden Rock and pick up a tank of propane. One time I was driving way too fast and when I turned the corner the tank rolled out and down a steep bank. It probably scared away all the rattlesnakes. I waited for it to blow up; when it didn't, I carried it up to the car. I was really strong then.

One time Ronnie, Art, and I went squirrel hunting. We cleaned the squirrel and roasted it over a camp fire; we ate a lot of squirrel hair but it was good. Another time we cooked potatoes in the coals and ended up with cremated potatoes. My dog, Chuck, loved to go squirrel hunting; even when we'd head home Chuck would try to lure us back into the woods for more hunting. When Chuck was born, he looked like a furry wood chuck. Mother named him Chuck.

There was a tree in the corner of our field. Lloyd recalled driving a nail into it; when the sawyer hit that nail we blamed it on trappers.

A man named Tiffany was very rich and owned a steam sawmill. Dad gave Arthur Hanson a good round oak heater. Old man Tiffany asked Mr. Hanson to take that heater with him to another job site. The Hansons were living in an old dance hall place. Mrs. Hanson expected me to keep the fire burning; all they had for wood was green piss elm; when it burns the flames are even cold.

Young Arthur always had a runny nose. Dad grabbed him one day and wiped his nose; Arthur was about 3 feet tall. He said when he grew up he was going to buy Dad out and pee on him. Arthur had a son named Tommy who was treated badly by the kids at the Elmwood School, so when he grew up he got even with all of them by beating them up.

One day when Lloyd was driving school bus no kids showed up at Arthur Hanson's. All at once young Arthur came climbing out of a barrel with no clothes on. It was 7 AM. When Lloyd went into the house, he found Arthur's dad sleeping off a hangover. The oldest boy, Tom, and I were good friends.

When Arthur Hanson died Mrs. Hanson asked Mr. Tiffany for help and Old Man Tiffany told her "he couldn't hear her." Onetime Old Man Tiffany had to appear in court; when the judge was going to fine him, he threatened to shut down all 3 mills; the case was dismissed.

When my dog, Chuck, was quiet we'd better see what he was up to. He liked to help Mother gather the chickens at night, and sometimes he liked chicken. When I had that big black Lab Nederhauser had given me some chickens; they'd been caged and didn't know how to be chickens. When my Lab stared at them some just died!

Dad liked to watch wrestling; Wilma did too. So many times, I'd end up outside adjusting the antenna! I'd use a pipe wrench and Dad would call out, "just a little more." Finally, no one came out of the house so I assumed they had the wrestling, and I had to go milk. Dad liked Howdy Doody too. Mom wasn't very happy about Dad's choices; she liked Perry Mason.

Dad and Don Heinze went fishing and somehow Dad fell out of the boat into the water. Grace gave Don all kinds of grief over that: "trying to drown my Dad." When Don would drive Dad places, he was always pointing out places he had wired (he was an electrician at Armors for years and locally too). Dad would get so disgusted hearing, "I wired that."

Donna was born on a beautiful spring day. Lloyd had gone to Maiden Rock looking for a grain drill that day. Donna was born that evening. I think I was 12 or 13. Maxine was born on the way to the hospital in the winter time. She and Donna were "contaminated babies" because they weren't born in the hospital. When Lloyd was filling out the admit forms for Grace to be in the hospital he asked the nurse, "what about the baby? "Lloyd said," you should have seen them scramble then." When Lloyd was washing out the back seat of the car he told Art and I to "get out of there." Alan was born on a bright October day. Lloyd stopped at our place and kicked Bernard and Art out and went down the road to Red Wing. Art and Bernard sat on the steps and kicked the dirt. I was so worried when Art was born that my brother wouldn't like me anymore.

David and Isabell were Chivareed at our house. Dad didn't go for all that nonsense. Mother made the best Banana Cream Pies and Pineapple Upside Down Cake. Lloyd would say they tasted like more and he got seconds. Mom's bread, cakes, and pies were delicious, and she cooked with a wood burning stove for years until we got a propane stove.

One time I burned the Smokehouse down. The neighbors came from miles around. I had a big cardboard tube and started a fire in it. I was playing then walked down to help Dad split wood. The mail man went by and saw the fire and sped down the road. Then our neighbor, Oscar, came up the road followed by other neighbors. Dad looked up and saw the smoke. He told me to "get into the house and shut up!" The Smokehouse was made out of Poplar and it was soaked in grease from all the meat Dad and Mother had smoked. And I didn't get punished. I was probably in 1st grade. It was a nice fall day. NOTE: One of their neighbors commented about Lyle's father: "He never saw a fire he didn't like even if it was on his neighbors place." In the years Lyle and I were together he would burn brush piles, dry grass, and dead tree limbs. On one occasion he had hauled a bunch of tree limbs and dead grass into the upper pasture. He was still outside when it started to get dark. I looked up into the field and he had set that stuff on fire, and it was getting away from him. The fire truck came up the driveway with the siren blowing. I stayed in the house; didn't know that guy! They helped him put the fire outand he didn't get fined.

Mother had all 9 children at home. Grandma Larson was the mid-wife except for me. A doctor from Maiden Rock delivered me at home. My brother, Robert, died when he was 2 months old. My older sister, Mabel, was living with Charlie Sticht; Grandma Larson brought her home so none of Charlie's kids would catch whooping cough. Mabel brought it to Robert. Dad could never find anything wrong with his mother so he blamed Mother for Robert's death. This really hurt their marriage. Mother became real bitter and started listening to radio religion. She did like Reverend Goswell at Ono Methodist. He was a very kind man.

The main part of our house was there in 1912. Jim McCrea said, "Let's tear that old kitchen lean to off and build a better kitchen." Jim put a window seat in the kitchen; it was a wonderful place for plants.

I paid for water to the house in 1962. Mother carried water to the house from up by the barn for years. It really bothered me that my mother had to carry water so far. She was a very tiny woman and worked so hard. Lloyd and Dad did a poor job of putting the line in. It wasn't deep enough; they could have bought a couple hundred feet of hose and done better. It should have been deeper, and if I'd been home I'd have dynamited the rock so it could have been buried a lot deeper.

Mother got a combination gas/wood cook stove in the late' '50's. I bought her a dryer when I came home on leave. I was drying my clothes at the base in California and thought, "Mother would sure like one of these." I had a man wire it in.

Dad bought a threshing machine then we had to have a tractor. Dad had always used a team to plow, harrow, plant, and mow. The 1st year we used Oscar Nelson's tractor. Dad had a Galloway engine he ground grain with and run a buzz saw. I liked to listen to the Galloway; it went "Chug A Chuga and then Bang Bang." Then Dad and Lloyd scrapped it!

Dad got his own tractor in 1951; he paid $700. for it, a plow, and cultivator. It was an International B with a wide wheel base so it wouldn't tip over on the hillsides.

Gas was always delivered early in the morning. Dad put it in a rusty old barrel so I got to be an expert on emptying the sediment bulb. The tractor would stop dead and I'd have to remove the sediment bulb and blow the line out.

When my dad was a small boy and was still living on Prairie Island, an old Indian Lady picked him up and held him over a fire by his feet. She was showing everyone how the Indians killed white children. One of the Suters said, "You probably killed a few yourself." Grandma Larson, Dad's mother, was a Suter.

When I was in the Military we had to practice for riots. The Sea Bees, in about 1959, had practiced on stopping riots. We could not imagine such a thing so we rioted against Santa Claus! "Down With Santa!" We were trained to use the upside-down V formation when going into the crowd. It worked well.

THE END of the notes; I sure wish I'd taken a lot more!

FAMILY IN PHOTOS

John David Suter and Annie Busch Suter
Lyle's Dad's maternal grandparents

Once In A Lifetime Comes A Man

Annie Busch Suter

Lyle's Dad's mother, Annie Suter Larson, 1 of 22 children

Lyle's Mother, Annie, front middle - Ebensperger family -Emil, Fred, John, Emma, Jacob, Bertha, Henry, Mother Caroline

Lyle's father, Robert Arthur Larson

Lyle's Mother, Annie back left, Aunt Bertha front center, Rein Sisters Emily & Gertrude

Lyle's Dad's Siblings: Uncle Julie's Wife,
Caroline, Mabel, Arthur, Julie
Lyle said his mother was so disgusted when
Julie's wife wanted in this picture.

Arthur Robert Larson

Uncle Julie

Larson Family: Lloyd, Lyle, Alice, Isabel,
Grace, Violet, Shirley, Mabel
Arthur and Annie in back

Arthur Robert Larson early 1970's

The Larson farm before the old barn was torn down and replaced just before the great depression of the 1930's.

Painting of the new barn by Lyle's nephew, Steven Olson

LYLE'S EARLY YEARS

THE "LOVE" OF my life, Lyle Larson, was born at home on his parent's anniversary January 1, 1936. He grew up on a small farm in Wisconsin.

Some photos of his early years:

Larson Farm

Once In A Lifetime Comes A Man

1947   1948

Lyle's mother had printed "My Son" on this photo.
Her love for him could be felt in these words.

NAVY SEA BEE

LYLE ENLISTED IN the Navy January 15, 1957. He served in Guam and Alaska. His favorite place was Kodiak, Alaska. All of his free time was spent hiking bear trails and fishing for salmon.

Lyle 's jobs were varied; dynamiter, carpenter, and concrete mason. His discharge was January 13, 1961 with a rank of E-5. He was very proud of his military service and used his Sea Bee skills throughout his life.

Once In A Lifetime Comes A Man

Once In A Lifetime Comes A Man

TIME

"LIFE HERE IS only a whisper in time" became a reality when Lyle passed away. All of the yesterdays we had are now a flash; 32 years flew by before our very eyes. So many things a person takes for granted; like we will always be together never thinking that one of us would have to walk on alone, and that someone happens to be me! A Blackfoot Indian Chief summed life up like this: "What is life? It is the flash of the firefly at night; it is the breath of a buffalo in the winter time; it is the little shadow that runs across the grass and loses itself in the sunset."

Change is always a constant in life and I've had to adapt so many times. This change has been the most difficult; months have passed since Lyle died. I still have lots of tears to shed along with so many wonderful memories. He was my Handsome Brown Eyed Man.

Once In A Lifetime Comes A Man

LOVE AT FIRST SIGHT

A COUPLE OF WEEKS before Lyle died, I asked him if there was such a song as "The First Time Ever I Saw Your Face." He said there was so I shared with him the first time I saw his face in 1957. I had married a man he grew up with. One day my husband said, "we are going to Arkansas, Wisconsin; my Buddy is home on leave." The place where we met Lyle was a bar with big round tables for seating, and a line of bar stools near the bar.

My husband was always the "life of the party" drinking and making the rounds to visit with everyone. I sat down at one of the big round tables. Soon Lyle came over and sat down across from me; that is how we met; no introduction at all as my husband was too busy visiting others in the bar. I looked across the table at the most handsome man I had ever seen! My heart did flip flops and I said to myself, "And you are married! It was love at first sight! Lyle asked me where his friend had found me; a girl who did not drink or smoke and was country. I don't remember what I answered as I was experiencing so many feelings; sadness and wanting to be free so I could spend time with Lyle and knowing I was married so a lot of Guilt!

And, young and ignorant, I was determined to make my marriage work. I was not going to be like my mother. She had been married so many times and my childhood were not the best even though today I value all the experiences from those years.

My husband's mother had arranged our marriage; she bought the ring and the dress. She was sure I could change her son. I was a 16-year-old girl looking for love in the wrong place!

At the time Lyle and I met I didn't know my husband's sister was married to Lyle's brother. Through the 8 plus years I was with him I would see Lyle occasionally. I helped some with haying at his brother's farm so was able to visit with Lyle then. Once he dared me to start a Caterpillar with the gas starting engine then switching it to diesel. I'd learned how to do this as a teenager because we used the Cat to run the hay chopper at my grandparent's sheep ranch. To Lyle's surprise I easily started the Cat. In later years he said back then all I talked about was how great Montana was, and he didn't like my "cat-eyed" glasses.

The night of the Caterpillar his nephew was with us so that special time was shared. We did have more time together when Lyle took our car to return a toy truck my husband had taken from a bar in Pepin. I got up the courage to tell Lyle I was in love with him. We parked and kissed; I can't recall where but Lyle pointed the spot out after we were married. After Robin was born Lyle had driven her and I to a doctor's appointment in Plum City. That was the last time we were together; that was October of 1964.

When I finally ended my marriage, I had 4 small children and Lyle had a girlfriend. My self-esteem was horrible bringing with those thoughts of how I wasn't good enough for Lyle anyway. I was a divorcee! My naiveté hadn't allowed me to use my ex's infidelity which began soon after we were married. Had I done so I could have been free, and wouldn't have even been pregnant with my oldest son. Hind sight is so enlightening and painful.

Painful can best be described by our grief over the years we could have been together and weren't. The last week of Lyle's life he was talking with a lot of sadness about how we missed our young years together. He was depressed over those memories and what might have been. Our lives had not come back together for almost 18 years.

Lyle was in my thoughts over the years but always with a sense of loss, sadness, and prayers for his health and happiness. He said he always thought about living in Alaska and the only person he thought he'd want to share that with was me. He didn't know I was scared to death of bear!

DESTINY

DESTINY HAD A hand in us being together after so many years. As I look back now, I can see God's Hand in bringing us together again. In 1981 I was going to college in Spokane and he was still farming in Wisconsin. I had a dream with Lyle and 2 boys walking up the bank to his house. One boy had dark hair and one light.

I had forgotten all about my dream until several months after Lyle's death. That is when I fully realized God had to have had a hand in our lives. The blond- and dark-haired boys were his great nephews. They had spent a lot of time with Lyle canoeing, fishing, and helping him on the farm. He said they were like sons to him.

The dream was so vivid. I started obsessing about Lyle; was he married? Did he have children? Was he even alive? After several days of trying to figure out how I could find the answers to these questions I decided to call his brother. I pretended to be an old navy buddy. No, he wasn't married and he was in good health. He gave me Lyle's phone number.

By the time I had enough courage to call him he'd already been told about the suspicious call; was it really from an old navy buddy? I can't remember what we talked about. Lyle had the most pleasing phone voice! We exchanged addresses and started our new found relationship through our letters.

When I was going through some of Lyle's personal items after he died, I found all the letters we'd written in a steel box. Also, his first haircut hair in an envelope dated November 11,1939. His sister had given him that haircut. On November 19, 2013 I gave Lyle his last haircut.

November of 1981 found both of us needing someone! We were lonely with lack of direction. Lyle was trying to keep his farm going and feeling very much alone especially Holidays and weekends. His father had passed away so he lived by himself. I was trying to get through college and earn a degree in Chemical Dependency Counseling. Dan and Robin were still at home but would soon be adults. We'd moved to Spokane from Anaconda, Montana so I could go to college.

LETTERS

ONE THING ABOUT distance it helps a friendship develop. One of my letters mentioned my job as an Inmate Paint Crew Supervisor. Lyle said he thought that meant I'd been in prison! Even so he'd continued writng and we'd call each other at least once a week. Phone calls were expensive then.

Lyle's Letters (1982):

March 5 "Thank you" for your letters. I look forward to getting them. Please feel free to write anytime you like. I work for the Post Office and your stamps help pay my wages. "He had just finished a book about the Lewis & Clark Expedition. "I would give up years of my life to have been with them when they saw this country in all its glory."

"Be careful of my sister-in-law; she thinks I shouldn't see girls." (That reminded me of her telling me years ago that Lyle should not see girls! That was another reason I gave up so easy. Knowing what I know now nothing would have stopped me; his sister-in-law, his girlfriend, or anyone else.)

Icky Cat and Bowser Dog were his companions. "Ick is very homely. She has a habit of hiding my pens and frequently my blood pressure medicine."

April 5, was about his work on a barge that went from Texas to Louisiana and his farm. He was in Louisiana during Mardi Gras.

His description: "Mardi Gras is one big drunk". He was fattening 25 steers with their average weight about 1300, had a few Suffolk sheep, and was no longer milking cows. He mentioned his love of poetry. "I used to know by heart all of The Raven and the Highway Man." Ick had his pen under the typewriter keys so no capitols in this letter.

April 8, "You will make no points with me running down Ronnie" (Ronald Reagan). I was what I call Unionized as I'd belonged to the Painter's Union and had been a union steward. It didn't take long for me to become a conservative once those unionized glasses came off much to Lyle's delight.

April 14, "My brother-in-law, Dean, had a heart attack. 53 years old! He is going to be okay."

The first thunderstorm. (We both loved to watch lightening play in the sky.) He was hoping the storm would bring lots of green grass. His neighbor had called; her mare foaled but the foal wasn't nursing. Even with vet care the foal died. Lyle didn't think it had milk in time to do it any good. When we had our own mares Lyle or I would milk the mare into a bottle then bottle feed the foal. That gave it strength and we could go back to bed without worry.

April 16, "Raining again. The grass has a little shade of green. My sheep are sure anxious to get to it. Thank you for typing and sending the poem," The Hunting Of The Snark "by Lewis Carroll." My belief about love. "When you are alone and see something beautiful you wish she were there to share it with you. When you see or hear something funny you want her there to laugh with you. This may seem dumb but it is my feeling about love."

In another letter he wrote, "I do remember kissing you and how good it was even though the kiss was hurried. It would have been even better with more time." (I also remembered the deep and intense feelings I had, and the sadness I'd felt through the years whenever I'd think of him.)

I asked him why he was still single. He replied, "I get bored with girls with small minds. All they ever talk about are pretty things and watch TV; never read a newspaper or a book. TV has to be the most boring of all."

We discussed religion and astrology. Lyle expressed doubt about the resurrection. And when astrology came up, he said, "My sign is the Goat and I hate goats." Mine isn't much better as I am on the cusp of the Scorpion and the Archer.

After we were married when we would go out to a Chinese Restaurant we'd have fun reading about our sign's meanings even though we'd take it all in with a grain of salt. Lyle was a Rat and I a Dragon. We observed that the Rat partnered well with the Dragon. Characteristics of the Rat: Intelligent, Adaptable, Quick-witted, Charming, Artistic, and Sociable. The Dragon: Lucky (and how lucky I was to be married to Lyle) Flexible, Eccentric, Imaginative, Artistic, Spiritual, and Charismatic. Lyle could certainly attest to my being Eccentric! He brought Balance to my life and he never had a dull moment as my husband.

April 19, "A long time dream is to canoe the Missouri River from Ft. Benton to Ft. Peck." That dream was realized when his nephews arranged the canoe trip in 2005. They brought their canoe from Wisconsin and loaded Lyle's when they got to our place. They had the entire trip planned from meals to overnight camping although their first night was spent in the historic Ft. Benton Hotel. This trip was a wonderful highlight in Lyle's life.

He liked Joseph Wambaugh's books and mentioned the Executioner's Song about Gary Gilmore's death by firing squad in Utah. The song Gilmore had chosen was Paloma Blanco (White Dove). When I started my own counseling business in 1994, we tried to come up with a logo and Lyle suggested the White Dove. That became the logo for my business. In 2013 Lyle said he would like this song played at his funeral when we were talking about our last wishes.

Other Wambaugh books he mentioned were "The Blue Knight" and "The Onion Field." He added, "Did I ever tell you that I find sports boring? I can't stand football. What I like best is canoeing."

Canoeing The Missouri River 2005

April 21, "I am preparing for sheep shearing. Twin lambs were born yesterday; the ewe and lambs died; fed the old bitch all winter then she dies 2 days before shearing. And I won't shear a dead sheep like the old sheep men did. I would throw up all over it. I hauled many loads of manure yesterday; my steers are happier now. They are full of ground corn, all they want to eat, and a little hay."

"Just read a book called" The Chariots Of The Gods "by a Swiss man, <u>Erich Von Daniken</u>. He tries to prove God is or was an astronaut; some of his ideas were disturbing. I do believe in life on other planets although not in our solar system. How the Ancients could make out lions, bulls, and such is more than I can see. I can make out the Dippers and the Cassiopeia constellation that is located in the northern sky, and the Pleiades. I dislike the city because one can't see the stars or the moonlight. I would rather have a telescope than any toy I can think of." (Which brings to mind the telescope I bought for him at a pawn shop. All that one could see were fly specks. What a disappointment as that was on the lens and the scope didn't work at all.)

April 22, "I like writing to you almost as much as getting your letters. That will slow down once spring works starts. Speaking of "sexy" reading your last letter was kind of an ego trip; never thought of myself as a Don Juan type. I am very shy around women and let them make the first move."

April 30, These words to a song have been going through my mind. "Are you going away with no word of farewell; will you leave not a trace behind; I could have loved you better; didn't mean to be unkind; believe me that was the last thing on my mind; it's a lesson to late for the learning; made of sand made of sand." I don't remember the singer but know it was a man. As I sat here eating potato chips and sour cream, I typed the words to this song out then thought I may as well start a letter to you. "(During the last weeks of Lyle's life he brought this song up again and said it always reminded him of those years we weren't together. We researched this and the song was Glenn Campbell's" Last Thing On My Mind.)

April 30 cont: "Got a good days work done today. Yesterday, had a flat tire on the plow so drove to Maiden Rock; I was too late. Damn Daylight Savings Time. I thought it was about 3 PM. So, I hurried to Cenex early this morning. The tire had a thorn stuck in it; pretty tough trees."

"Bernard's brother-in-law's wife saw a bear near here yesterday, and on my land. I think bear eat sheep? No TV tonight. I took my lead in wire down because it comes in across the field I am plowing. No car here at the house either. I took it to Bernard's to get his tractor and grain drill, so here I sit on a Friday night. I could take the truck to town; as my buddy would say, "drink beer and talk smart."

I had a friend in the Navy who would say "drink beer and swap lies." My buddy had another saying, if someone called a girl a bad name, "That doesn't make her all bad." Last time I saw him he was drinking 2 twelve packs a day and his wife was leaving him. When I tried to talk to him he said he liked beer. When I think of all the alcoholics, I know I could keep you busy right here."

"Did you know that astronomers believe that on the other side of the black hole there may be a white hole with matter spilling into another universe? I have always liked stars. The best place to see them is from a raft out on the lake. I had a girl friend in Eau Galle; on hot August nights we would swim out to a raft, lay on our backs, and watch falling stars. I quit going with her because she drank too much. She could drink me under the table and most nights she ended up helping me into her house. Her mother would get me up and make breakfast. She was a nice friend but more like a sister. This must be my night for reminiscing."

"I went over your last letter to see if you had any questions. The one on the water from Duluth; that water goes north. It doesn't run into the Mississippi. The Mississippi is much cleaner than you remember it. One can eat fish without concern now. Remember the time I caught fish and brought them to Lloyd's?

That was the night I bet you couldn't start a Caterpillar.

"Remember the time I met you in Maiden Rock. You were after Velvet for your husband. When you saw me, you gave it to Helen to take to him. You and I were so dumb; we went to Bay City. Why did we go to Bay City? I drank more in those days. Remember the toy truck your husband stole from the bar in Pepin and didn't have the nerve to take it back? You went with me in your car when we took it back."

"I'm trying to change my lifestyle and not worry so much about getting crops in, etc. If I get far behind, I will just go fishing. It is late, 10:30 already and Ick just came in from her day of hunting chipmunks, dodging cars, and dogs. She has really changed her lifestyle; stays out all day and sleeps all night."

"Cigarettes went up a nickel and the DUI laws are a lot stricter. And of course, WI has a sales tax. Oh yes, I picked up some Vitamin C. Had a phone call from my nephew's wife; we talked for almost an hour. I went to bed but didn't sleep very well. I was too tired; woke up with Ick laying on my neck. It's bright and sunny; gotta get my cows fed."

PS: "I took 3 Vitamin C and don't feel any different. Ick is gone for the day. She's trying to catch robins that are as big as partridge." May 4, "The first thunderstorm of the season drove me in from the field. I'm about 2/3 done planting. Cindy and I walked the pasture last evening; I think I found a bear track. The track was as big as my hand. Later we sat and drank up my left-over wine. Cindy read your poems; she liked them."

"I have to get the air conditioner fixed; this place is like a tin sweat box. The county widened the road and cut most of the nice shade trees; dutch elm did the rest in. I believe the way the land is being paved over and used to build houses we will see real hunger before we are too much older; may have to protect a garden. I never plant one anymore; too busy in the fields and the weeds get ahead of me. Same thing with mowing the lawn; my lawn is the talk of the neighborhood. The only time I have off it rains; before long the grass is a foot tall. I have a self-propelled walking lawn mower, "More like a dead run."

"My great nephew joined the Navy. He is as close to a son as I have ever had. He is a student at the University of Minnesota ROTC.

He wants to be a Navy pilot. I hope he doesn't make it! Way too dangerous if we get into another war. He is coming next Sunday with his girl friend. We plan to canoe the Chippewa River from Durand to Nelson. It's about 20 miles."

"Nora called; she swears a lot as she tells me all of her troubles. I just let her talk and make tea, go to the bathroom, etc. She never notices that I am gone. She is very pretty but her language puts me off. Why she confides in me I don't know. I seem to have that trouble, "women telling me things that they never even tell their husbands." "Today is my 5th day on Vitamin C and I still feel the same. What is it good for again? Icky just came in all wet. I haven't had supper yet or dinner for that matter. I got myself a dish of ice cream & Ick is sharing that with me."

"Last Sunday I planted oats at my brother's. By mistake I planted the corner of their garden spot; did Grace ever get mad. I almost didn't get supper. I really must do something about my eyes; need reading glasses now. Sorry about my last letter; I wasn't drunk, just depressed."

May 7, "It rained all day, couldn't get in the field so I was fencing. I cut my finger so bad my glove finger filled up with blood. This Japanese typewriter, the ribbon is running out. I hope you don't mind red ink.

The darn sheep got out; as I was running after them, I started coughing so bad my elbows hurt.

Cigarettes!"

"I have a Chet Atkins record, "White Silver Sands" that I play a lot. I think Don Rondo made it popular. I am fickle when it comes to music. When I was in the Navy, and at a bar in California, I played "Gotta Travel On" by Billy Grammer so many times I got kicked out of the bar."

May 9, "Got your letter and card today. I guess I don't want to live where you can see snow on the mountain year around. 5 months out of the year is enough for me. I think I got a raise at the Post Office. My eyes are so bad the letters look blurred on this typewriter. And I can't find my cigarette papers.

Damn Cat. I never did get the sheep in either; they are still eating my winter wheat and talking smart. Is marriage work or play? I heard a joke about that once and will tell it to you someday. I'm so tired guess I'll have a cup of tea. Mr. Coffee went nuts this morning so the heck with that; besides that tea is less of a mess."

"This letter is kind of choppy; just writing thoughts as they come. I have my pickup fixed; went to the junk yard and got parts and stole a few more. A friend used to say, "It is human nature to steal from a junk yard."

"The moon is really bright tonight so no sleep. When I was young I would look at the full moon and get a yearning to travel. It just pulled at me. Now all I get is less sleep. I still can't find the cigarette papers but I did find my pipe."

May 12, "If I only write to you when it rains it looks like I will be writing a lot of letters. I worked late last night plowing, harrowing, and planting. I saw the largest falling star ever. It went behind a thunderhead and the glow of it lit the western sky for a few seconds. 3 deer crossed in front of my tractor lights; they looked as big as elk." "Nora just called. Her sheep died; smart sheep. In a half hours' time she called me an s.o.b., a dumby, and a wise guy. I think she likes me. She wants me to help her on her house; no way!"

"I brought the baby lambs in as it started to rain again. Then I backed up to the feed mill and started grinding feed. I have to go through the sheep lot to get to the steer pen. As I got off to shut the gate I fell in the mud! Then the sheep saw their chance and zoom 30 sheep ran past in a flash flinging mud on me. The sheep headed for my newly sprayed oats and started eating. "Oh, for a good dog." Then as I backed the feed mill up a steer got out. As I was trying to get him in another one got out. It was still pouring rain so I gave up for a while."

"Cindy, her friend, and I went canoeing. I'd varnished the paddles that morning; before we even got started, Carrie rubbed her eye and got varnish in it. Then Cindy got it in both eyes; we started as soon as Cindy got that washed out. I sat in the middle and let the girls paddle. If I added their ages together it is 47 one year older than I am. They paddled while I fished and caught snags; the river was high, almost a half mile wide. The wind came up strong enough to cause white caps. Carrie screamed. I paddled to the right bank where the wind wasn't so bad but as soon as we stopped paddling, we went backward, or worse in circles. We stopped near a little town called Ella for beer, and to see how far we had to go. No beer in Ella; we had come 12 miles and had 10 to go. Carrie fell in the river; it was over her head and cold. Then we got into a lot of trees; with the roots still in the bank where they go up and down, not a good thing to canoe over in a river. Cindy must've steered us into a dozen of them. Carrie was a big help; she screamed every time we hit one. Cindy got her hand on some garbage and called the river a damned old sewer. She had two shots of whiskey when we got back to Durand then broke out in a rash. I drove home and went fishing with Bernard's boy. We caught some nice sunfish. The next morning, I woke up and rubbed my eyes; wow, did it burn. It had something to do with that varnish I put on the paddles."

"Carrie's quite the girl. When she got out of high school she went to Gillette and Rock Springs, Wyoming to work construction on and off for three years. She made herself up like a boy to get the jobs and never got fired. Although she said she did get some pretty bad work just for fooling them. That was before civil rights and ERA."

"Monday, I went to fix fence and the track came off my crawler. Will let the cows out to pasture tomorrow; the grass has a good start and it has stopped raining. I'm going out to see if anymore lambs have been born. I wish I could get out of this farming but the job market looks very bad."

"It's strange how people like different parts of the country; you didn't like it here and Cindy loves it so much she sings country roads, and uses western Wisconsin instead of West Virginia. I have never given it much thought. I liked Texas and Montana; just so it isn't flat land. I don't like real flat ground because it's too windy." (And where did he end up living for over 30 years? Eastern Montana. Beautiful sunsets though and one can see forever into the horizon.)

"How's this for closing "yours till Niagara Falls", Love Lyle PS: got a letter from you today."

May 14, "Thanks for letting me out of the reception for John's 90 plus birthday. Your ex blamed me for your break up, no use adding to it."

"Friday afternoon, I got the sheep in about dark and had to carry 4 lambs while the mothers ran around in the mud. Got bored so went to Dean's bar and stayed until closing time; just sat and talked and sipped Dean's warm beer. I saw a beaver in the road on the way to town. I was going to run over it but couldn't because he or she had a front paw missing. I leaned out the car window and it stood and hissed at me. I pulled my head back in real fast."

"Saturday, I spread the last load of manure. When I opened the gate the little lambs got under the tractor; as I was getting them out, zoom, they were all gone. Bet they had it all planned. For 2 cents I would put them all out on pasture and let them take their chances. " "I'm eating warmed up chow mein. A sheep had a big lamb born dead; she won't leave it; just stands there looking at it and bleating.

Another ewe had a lamb so small it was the size of a rat; it is still living. I have caught her twice and fed the lamb; it might make it." "I was teasing you about vitamin C; you haven't caught on to my weird humor; some never do. I am seldom serious about anything.

There is nothing in life to get too worked up about; most things work out by themselves and we will all end up dead anyway."

"Why did you marry an Indian anyway? I don't have much use for the ones that sit around and moan about their lost land, and use that for an excuse to drink. The one on TV cries when he sees litter; he should go to a reservation where he could cry a river over all the litter. Aren't I nasty today; it must be the weather? A navy buddy and I were in a bar in Great Falls, Montana with 12 indians. They made me nervous but my buddy said if I couldn't lick 6 of them, I wasn't a man. He was Montana born and raised."

"I went out to plow and was on the far end of the field when it started to rain. All I had on was a T-shirt; now I am shivering. I wish I hadn't gone because Bob left me a note. Bob and Steve are brothers; both like sons to me. He and his wife were here on their way back from Maryland; he is a lieutenant in the USN and a nuclear physicist. They are on their way to Pearl Harbor and his first Submarine. And my house is a mess; the best way to have company is don't clean the house."

"I went to Bernard's to get my dog; forgot her there yesterday. There were all kinds of excitement when I got to Bernard's. He had a cow in the woods that couldn't calve. I helped him pull the calf but the cow would not get up. He called the vet; the cow had a broken pelvis. Then my nephew came as I was leaving; he'd been drinking and started bitching over some long ago forgotten thing. I and my dog, Bowser, got in my car and went home. He won't come near my car when Bowser is in it. She gets mean when she's in the car. She bit Steve when we were duck hunting. She got in the car and when Steve got in and reached for the keys she got upset."

"When I got home, I fed the rat sized lamb. I was so sweaty I took a shower; what I need is a shower curtain. Can't find my cigarettes. A man just called for hay and I don't have any. Now Nora is talking to me on the phone; I will keep on typing till she catches on. She has a 12 pack and wants me to meet her halfway to drink it. No go, when I drank last night that was it; one hangover at a time. She hung up with a bang. A couple of years ago she pulled a gun on me and was going to shoot me then herself. I had to talk long and low to get her to put it back. I almost brought myself to sleep talking."

RAIN AND HUMOR

"THE RAIN WASHED all the plum blossoms off but I've never seen so many violets. They are in the road ditches, the house yard, and they give me a good reason for not mowing the grass. What a day; first my nephew chews me out then Nora calls me names. If Dan likes to read let him try The Right Stuff by Tom Wolfe."

"Now I'm going to try to tell you about my sense of humor. Here goes; years ago, I spent a lot of time and charm trying to get this nameless girl to go out with me. After a long time and many ideas, I couldn't even be serious. The more I thought about all the time and money I'd spent on her the funnier it seemed. I got to laughing so hard I scared her and that struck me as funny too. I still think it's funny but she doesn't. Another time I was with this girl in St. Paul. She wanted to dance in the rain; when we broke up that winter I said, "you mean we will never dance in the rain? "She snapped back," not with you anyhow." I started laughing as she got madder and madder. She called me weird and said she was glad to get rid of me. I just laughed some more; never saw her again. If I was rich I would shoot those damn sheep. Love, Lyle"

PS: "when you are back here you may hear stories about Cindy and myself; not true we are friends and will stay just friends."

Sunday, May 15, "What a day, rain followed by more rain, lots of thunder and lightning, and more rain coming tomorrow. To make things worse Bernard and I went to town last night. I have been so sick; no more beer for a while. The weather is getting me down. I did get quite a lot of plowing done yesterday. I slept most of today." "The sheep have quit having lambs and the little rat lamb can suck on his own. Did you ever hear Johnny Cash's song "Forty Shades Of Green?" That is what it looks like now. The real light new green leaves against the older darker green leaves. The air has a soft feel not found at any other time of the year. I can't find enough words to describe how the land looks and the air feels. Here I sit with a hangover and all I can think of is sleep. Mark Twain went bankrupt publishing his own books; so, take that fact and feel it." (I was writing a book)

"Do I ever wish you could see the beauty around me right now. The clouds are parting and rays of sunshine are hitting the ground making a veil affect. After a day of storms, the setting sun may oft be seen again. My mother used to say that for both the weather and for troubled times in life."

"I went to my nephew, Bernard's, to borrow some bread; his son, who is 13, backed the pickup into my car, broke the headlight, and rumpled the fender. At least it was on the rusty side; it's an old car so nothing to get upset about. I will have to get it fixed though."

Note: Lyle was very close to Bernard's son. He often spoke of taking him fishing and his love of the song, Rhinestone Cowboy. From the time he was old enough to go with him Lyle would take him every chance he got. He said one time he, Bernard, and Bernie were driving on a country road; a pickup was off the road and stuck. Lyle said Bernie hollered in his ear, "Is he stuck!" Bernie went on to become a Sea Bee which made his uncle, Lyle, very proud.

"Wish I had the strength to make something to eat; no wonder, grapefruit is all I have eaten in 24 hours. If I keep living alone, I will die of starvation. I'm heating up some soup; maybe that will help me feel better."

"It is raining again. The robins are loving this weather. Worms have to come up or drown; the robins are getting fat but if the rain doesn't stop there won't be any apples because the bees can't work." "I have a Marty Robbins record on the Strawberry Roan. That damn mare of Cindy's tried to run me down when I went to get my tractor out of shed that's on the place she rents. She said the mare was just playing but when she ran at me, I hit at her with my cap. She reared up on her hind legs but backed off."

"There is an 18-year-old girl that has a crush on me; it is embarrassing. She is nice to talk to and I asked her why not boys her own age? She said they are a scruffy lot. Do you know this song by

Hank Snow, "The Long Ride?" it is sad; we used to play it when I was in the Navy and cry. This is getting to be one of those depressing letters. Maybe it's because I've got so many Johnny Cash records about lost loves. Soon it will be midsummer night; I like to go up on the hill and watch the daylight as long as I can."

May 21, "Friday I got two letters from you. The vitamin C isn't helping my cold. The rat lamb died just when I thought he was going to be alright. My sister, Grace, was here with her grandson, Bob, my great nephew who is a Lieutenant. She was upset about my lawn and said she won't be back until it's mowed. I told her I would see her next winter."

"Grace, my sister-in-law, thinks I have a bleeding ulcer. I will ask Dr. Springer next week. It's another dark and cloudy day. I'm having my first cup of tea."

PS: "Have to work the mail route June 19th. Will you be here?"

May 22, "I'm eating Maple Nut ice cream and poking this typewriter with one finger. I had one finger hurt today and almost lost it; it hurts so bad I almost wish I had. What a day; thought I'd have a Pepsi. The can opener fell in the cat dish full of sour milk because the cat is gone so much. I bent the point on the combine and got that fixed. To heck with more field work today. I'm going to have a Pepsi and pizza for supper. What a smell; my sister told me to clean my oven in 1977 and I haven't gotten around to it yet. The pizza is called Tombstone; well named as the crust is hard as marble."

May 26, "Nora was here with plans for her house. I found this poem in her house plans. She got mad when I told her I was sending it to you."

I got my name on the singing birds
that mate when the spring is new
But I won't be selfish with all of these
I'll share them with you

"It it is 9 o'clock and I am really tired. I took 1 ulcer pill, 2 blood-pressure pills, and a vitamin C. I have one sister who takes 19 pills a day so I have a way to go. A rare thing happened today; that ewe that had the little rat lamb adopted another lamb all by herself. The lamb was a twin and wasn't doing too good, so things worked out swell."

May 27, "It's too wet to work so Bernard and I went to the junkyard to get a part for my truck. After working an hour and a half to get it off it was the wrong one. I was going to put the sheep out on pasture but the lambs were playing; they all formed a group, run around, and wouldn't come near the ewes so I gave up. I went out to put the track on the crawler, got it on alright but forgot the master pin at home.

It was so nice out I just sat and talked to my cows until it got dark. I didn't get a lot of work done today and a letter from you. Thank you."

June 9, "I am writing this because I told you I would write. I got your letter from the 5th today. I am not as slim as I look; can't seem to suck my belly in anymore. I wish there was an easy way to lose that bulge. I'm really looking forward to seeing you. You may not get this until you're back in Spokane. Drive with care as I want to see you badly. I will try to be by the phone on the 15th."

WISCONSIN BOUND

COLLEGE WAS OVER until July 5th. My son, Dan, and I planned our trip to visit my daughter and son but most of all so I could see Lyle again! I told him I'd be there on June 15th and even the time. He was surprised when I arrived just when I said I would. We'd gone through Yellowstone Park on our way and had traveled 1542 miles with all the sightseeing.

Nora had been trying to talk Lyle into marriage and she happened to be at his place when we arrived. I hadn't seen Lyle for 18 years so wanted to make a good first impression. My weight was ideal, my hair long and wavy, and the dress I had on very feminine. I don't know how soon she left but she didn't stay long enough to be introduced.

We spent the day visiting and I let Dan take the car to visit his aunt and family near Diamond Bluff and Red Wing. My vacation was 2 weeks long and every minute of every day was spent together. I don't remember when he proposed. This took place a few days after I arrived at his place. I do remember telling someone at Dean's Bar in Maiden Rock that we were going to be married. Again 32 years later I cannot remember his proposal. Too many stars in my eyes and a foggy brain.

We spent the days haying, talking, visiting his family, and with his dog Bowser. I would accompany him on his mail route. After dark we would go up in the field and look up at the constellations.

Lyle could name so many of the stars and planets; his knowledge and remarkable mind always amazed me. He would have been a fantastic science or history teacher. Bowser thought we were really losing it when we were laying on the ground looking up at the stars. She would run around us then come over and check us out. It took a little while before she settled down and accepted the idiosyncrasies of her humans.

When it comes to error, I am a real Klutz. When I was trying to put the key in the ignition of his car I managed to get it stuck. Patiently, Lyle fixed that mistake. Next, I tried to open his field glass case and tore the strap. Again, he repaired my overzealous opening job.

Lyle had asked me to drive the pickup home so he could bring the tractor from the lower field. I had not been back in that country for so long and I'm usually lost anyway! Each time I'd drive by the road to his place Bowser would turn her head and look. After doing this at least three times I finally took a hint from Bowser and turned up the correct road. I can get lost in my own back yard!

I make it sound like we didn't have disagreements or problems but we did. We planned a trip to Red Wing to see my mother, and again I was lost; as I kept trying to give Lyle my lost directions, he kept getting very impatient. After a few words I decided to keep quiet while he was driving. With little help from me he found his way to Mom's.

One evening we had agreed to meet my son and his fiancé for dinner at the Hilltop. As usual when I am nervous my brain is not in gear. I handed Lyle some money across the table to help pay for dinner. He was so embarrassed! I got a piece of his mind when we were by ourselves.

A note I wrote to Lyle when I was at his place: "Lyle, I love you and miss you. (I don't know where he had gone when I wrote this.) One of the cows was out. The neighbor down below called and said she was in his garden. I took the Farmall tractor and brought her home. She's in the corral. I hope she was the only one out. Cindy came after her horse. She hadn't seen any more cows so let's hope the 1 cow is it. I found some cigarettes in your red coat too. I write in my journal but even those words don't describe the wonderful joy of being with you. Lyle, I am the happiest woman in the world and I'm looking forward to being your wife. See you about 4; we are supposed to be at the Hilltop by 5.

My Handsome Brown Eyed Man Summer Of 1982

VACATION IS OVER

TIME WENT WAY too fast. I had to be back for summer classes and Dan had a job waiting for him. I barely gave us enough time to make the trip back on time. Lyle and I already had my next visit planned, and I would fly. He would pick me up at the Mpls/St. Paul Airport in late August.

As Dan & I were driving home to Spokane the following words kept going through my head so I decided to have them made into a song:

The Lovin's Somewhere In Between

Life begins with birth - It ends with death
The Lovin's Somewhere In Between
Alone I walked - Alone I ran
with your love branded upon my soul
Lessons for the learning
Days and nights of pain
No one for sharing
Until I heard from you again
Now together we walk
Together we run
With our lives in
the Lovin' Somewhere In Between
Your love branded my soul years ago

> With a brand that made the dying easier
> And life worth the living In
> The Lovin' Somewhere In Between

I sent a card to Lyle after my first trip to spend time with him: The caption: "I missed so much beauty before you!" This is what I wrote inside: "Even though I miss you and want to be by your side knowing that this parting won't last long allows sunshine in my vision and beauty in my days. Each hour passing by brings you closer; each sight I see brings thoughts of you. The wonder of our love fills the empty space; it awakens all my feelings and makes life worth the living. I Love & Miss You. Grace DUK "

Lyle said I was calm on the outside but my mind was going all the time; like a duck, calm on the surface and paddling like mad underneath. He nicknamed me DUK.

SUMMER LETTERS

Lyle's letters began on July 4th:

"ANOTHER BEAUTIFUL DAY that I wish I could share with you. Put up some excellent hay yesterday; now need to get it in the barn. That is the worst part. Your ex-sister-in-law, Grace, (also Lyle's sister-in-law) told me that I couldn't find a better wife if I spent the rest of my life looking."

"You must be on the road as I write this. My thoughts are with you of course that when you get this you will be safe at home. Bernard's family had fireworks so went up there then to Lloyd's for more fireworks. Cindy gave us 6 more glasses (Cenex). God, it was nice of you to call but can't you make it shorter? It is nice to hear you say you love me but I already know that; have no doubt of that fact. My sister, Alice, told me she is glad I am marrying you. Says it will be the best thing that's ever happened to me."

July 6: "My darling, my darling, love of my life; one day nearer becoming my wife. 2 letters from you with one post marked Jamestown, ND; the other Havre, MT. Both have been read several times and will be again."

"I've been cutting hay but it started to rain so Ick and I are having a tuna fish supper. When Cindy and I were in Dean's Bar I told her you were my one true love. The only time I wish I lived on a hill is when it storms. I love to see the dark clouds roll and the wind bend the grass and trees. Wish I could write love letters like you; all I can do is think of sweet things to say and you never remember them. Name one? I love you, Grace. I have never felt this way about anyone. Others that I thought I loved don't even seem real now; that must be what they mean by "puppy love". I hate being apart from you and speak to you in my mind constantly. Ick and I are going to take a nap as we were up at 5. Try sleeping on top of the covers with 2 flies in the room; you get up at daylight alright."

"Some nap 11 hours. Today was a lovely day; the air is cooler with some rain. Started back on 2 blood pressure pills. No letter today so I'm too sad to write anymore. It is one day nearer to holding you. Take good care of yourself as you belong to me."

In my July 7th letter to Lyle: "It must be nice to be a cloud; you just go where the wind pushes you, get to rain on picnics or not rain at all, be all white and fluffy one day then black and angry the next, and when you are tired of living you just dry up and go away."

July 9: "A long hot, muggy day but all days without you are long. I'm busy with the mail route and will harvest the wheat soon. This afternoon I went down to Dean's Bar. Ole Pappy asked about you and if I was really getting married. Adan, the alky, got you mixed up with Cindy which is just what I wanted. He also got the bartender mixed up. Dean tried to help and I left them in mass confusion."

"40 days till I see you again; 1 month and 10 days God willing. Bowser and I found a big dead rat. The poison is working and we put some more out. When I clean the barn, I want Bowser by my side if I have to tie her there."

"More about the wedding. It looks like I will be a stranger at my own wedding. Also, you are getting at least one short nightgown if I have to steal one. I love you and miss you; even missed you when you were out of sight when you were here."

"I hate owing people. Guess I'm depressed because I hoped the crops would help pay the bills but if it doesn't rain soon no crops; hate to write stuff like this to you but when I write it seems like I am talking to you and it helps somehow, and it may make you understand when you don't get a ring, or if only a small one. It's only 61 out so cold for this time of year. I love you the most; more with each passing hour and that is a fact."

"Listening to "Help Me Make It Through The Night." I want to help you through life and beyond if it is possible hope these letters don't bore you. I just set here and work away and write whatever is on my mind. I told Mrs. Holman that I was quitting the end of

November. She says "are you really getting married; she must be an unusual type of girl." She is."

July 10: "I had a good day today after I called you I won't call again until next Sunday. It was wonderful to hear your voice. I love you. Will you marry me? Now you have it in writing. I found a poem that I tried to tell you about. My sister Shirley knows it; it is called "The Death Of The Flowers." Good night Darling. Take care if I would lose you, I would die.

My reply July 12th: "my dearest Lyle your letter came today and I sure love what you said and how you said it. I am excited and happy and very grateful to become your wife. I am missing you. I can hardly stand the time away from you. My thoughts are with you constantly and today I missed the turn and held up traffic. Oh well that will help others learn patience. I do drive extra careful for you though; setting too long at an intersection or driving past the street I was to turn on isn't too dangerous."

Lyle wanted to know more about Spokane: "that clipping of Spokane is the IMAX theater and the pavilion that is in Riverfront Park. It looks out over the falls of the river; it is a beautiful park. The IMAX theater shows films of Mount St. Helens and other places. There is an interesting museum with all different geological finds. There is a rink for both ice and roller-skating, little cars for kids, etc. And the most beautiful merry-go-round I've ever seen. I will take some pictures myself, and also get some from the Chamber of Commerce to bring back. they may have some air shots that will show the mountains here better than any photo unless I took one from high drive. I can see down over trees and the valley to the distant mountains at the other end of the valley. Spokane is sort of built both on the mountain where we live and in the valley. The climate is pretty good here in the winter; milder than any other place I have lived. North of here is lots of lakes, streams, and timber. It is an awful lot like Idaho and western Montana here. I would like for us to someday go north up into Canada and see that country, and on over to the Banff area above Glacier Park. I don't care where I live as long as it is with you; it could be the north pole or the desert. I love you so much."

Okay, you told me how beautiful I looked when I came to see you. You told me how wonderful I felt. How very much you love me and I can't remember the others, and I hope you keep saying them forever anyway. You have placed me in heaven so far. How am I supposed to remember except the wonder of our love? It is now 39 days until I get on that plane and within three hours I will be in your arms and by your side.

Lyle's letters continued:

July 13: "This will be a short letter as it's already 10 o'clock. My nephew's back from Montana and he helped me hay last night then we went to Dean's and had a couple of seven ups. Can't tell you how sorry I am about the tone of last night's letter. (I didn't notice a negative tone) I took a bath, went to bed, had a long talk with myself, and found out what was troubling me. Most of it is that I am lonesome for you and can't seem to tell you how much I care for you in my letters. I was mad at myself for that. Please send me a picture of you no matter how bad you think it is. I don't have one of you and want one badly. I have been looking the marriage vows over and like them all; maybe we weren't the first people to be in love because whoever wrote them must've had a lot of feelings for someone. We will pick them out when you get here."

"Nora told this guy in Bay City that she waited too long and lost me to a tall beautiful woman. You are the light of my life now; when you left my life was left in darkness. I walked alone under dark stars soon to be right by your return. How's that for off-the-cuff at 10 AM? I don't get any house work done as I would rather write to you. I read all your letters at least 10 times."

July 13 again: "It is 12 hours nearer the time I will see you again. You are right about work making time go by faster. Thank you for calling this morning; don't remember much of what you had to say except for August 20. Last night the northern lights were really good; I hope for a repeat tonight. The radio said they were the best ever. Here is how I spend my day; I read your letter twice, go to the barn, pile 50 bales of hay, unload 50 more, go to the house, make lemonade, read your letter again then back to the barn for another 50. I may take Bernard's wife and the kids swimming. When we are married, we will have more time to talk things over. I told you that you were getting more beautiful every day and it was love that brings out your beauty. You are the only person that can call at 4 o'clock in the morning and make me too happy to sleep afterwards. The mailman will be early so I better get this in the mailbox. I love you, miss you, and you are always on my mind."

NOTE: I married Lyle's sister-in-law's brother on July 13, 1957. I was 16. Anyway, that is why I was in Wisconsin and met the love of my life, Lyle.

July 14: I am having tea and a toasted cheese sandwich. I finally got into the house by 9 PM. About the writers' conference, Grace, you can do anything that you want to; you are just as good as the next person. I have faith in you and I am proud of you win, lose, or draw. I love you madly. What did we learn from this week's news? That the Queen sleeps alone; how about that? Where was old Phil? Under the bed? Tell Dan that I think 20th century history is the pits; all good things ended with the Civil War."

July 15: "I am writing this as I clean house. It is raining so hard I bet the wheat lays flat; the wind must be 30 miles an hour. It may rain a lot when you are here but I think we can find something to do. Darling, I want to spend the first just holding and kissing you. It hurts really bad in my chest to think of it now; got to stop thinking about it and maybe the days will go faster. You must have a time reading these letters; I know I do. I just pound away and never look. Please keep your letters coming as I live for them, and I'm glad you are finding time to read. I think reading is better than all the movies and TV put together. About my blood pressure will go to the doctor next week and let you know. I hope he'll soon find one that will work so I can get a year's supply and won't need to be going to different doctors all time."

"Grace is talking about taking the train out to our wedding. Maybe you could work on her when you are here? The Rose is a lovely song but why take wonderful words like that and use that god-awful music. The sun is setting, the air is much cooler, the toads are croaking, and the robins are strutting around the yard like they brought the rain all by themselves. Must be nice to be a cloud just go where the wind pushes you, get to rain or not rain at all. This is the last of my paper I said more than I've said in 20 years. I love you Darling; my wife to be brings chills up my back; just thinking about you being my wife; a good feeling. You probably won't get this until Monday and if we talk Sunday, you will know it all anyway. But I do like writing to you. I could not live in a world that didn't have you. All my love and hugs."

July 19: "Today is a three-letter day. I ran out of typing paper and found this tablet along with a check to Wayne Morrow. What do I do with it? It's all ready to mail. (This was my rent check that I thought I had sent) Sunday morning I was so sick that I'm not even sure you called. I went back to sleep until noon then my nephew got me up as he was hungry and couldn't find his wife. How do you like my penmanship? I don't think I have ever been so sick from a cold but the mail must go and I have had to put up. I got a lot done by myself so just call me the little red hen. You better get the time and flight number to me again just in case I forget. I wrote you a long letter last night then tore it up this morning. We have been apart about all that I can take. But I do think the last 10 days will go faster; at least last time they did. Well, this will slow your letter reading down." July 20: I made it to the doctor today and my blood pressure is fine. When you are here you can test my blood pressure with your tester and if it goes up, I can take a pill or two. The basis for my plan is to get my blood pressure down with no salt. Smoking is the cause so, I quit Sunday.

NOTE: We both wrestled with cigarettes until 1988 when we quit for good. They caused many fights as we each sneaked cigarettes after we promised to quit. I understand now how afraid Lyle was of how badly they were affecting his health. He had open heart surgery October 16, 1989. If we hadn't quit in November of '88 he probably would not have lived to have that surgery.

July 21: "No letter today. This is as far as I had written when you called last night. Not much happening for news today we had a nice three-hour rain; it was raining when I got home from work so I took a nap. The sun came out so I took the rotary cutter out and cut weeds in the pasture. It looked so nice that I didn't stop until it was dark. The sheep seem happy and all that. I think some of my sheep are out but it's too late to do anything about it now."

"Sheep are running back and forth on the road dodging cars how will I get any sleep tonight. Today I wanted a cigarette so bad; It is day four. I can do it darling for you. I can't think of anymore to write. I sent for a present for you to use while you are here, I can use it too. Good night Darling; See you in less than two weeks; can't wait to hold you and kiss you.

July 29: "Well, I have a letter from you today. I have to start combining the wheat."

July 30: "One week from today; I will be so excited that I will be running around in circles. Oh, to have you in my arms again. It is a dandy day. I combined wheat yesterday; it rained a little so I took a load to Durand. I should finish it today. It is going 32 bushels per acre. Lloyd says that is good by Montana standards. It runs almost 100 per acre here in a good year. I got a wonderful letter from you yesterday; thanks for the star chart. It is supposed to be 90 above tomorrow so I think I will go swimming. If Cindy gets back, we may go sailing but the wind must be just right for that. I still miss those damn cigarettes and it will be two weeks Sunday. This will be my last letter to you as I will talk to you later then if I write to you, you may not get it anyway. I thought I would take some photos of the wheat harvest. I'm going to grind feed today. Say I didn't get a letter yesterday. Ick is about ready to have her kittens; I can feel the kitties inside of her and she looks like a basketball. I'm very happy that you will be here soon."

WISCONSIN AGAIN

AUGUST 6,1982: LYLE met me at the airport. I made it but my luggage didn't but we were able to pick it up in Red Wing the next day.

The following are from my journal:

August 10, it's been four days since I've had a cigarette. I want to smell nice and be healthy, and able to enjoy every moment God grants me with Lyle. I love his consideration and caring. These are things I've never known before. I look back and now I know that had I opened up to him 20 years ago I would have had the caring love then. Tears of joy come sweeping along so often because I just never thought I'd know his arms or his love ever again. No one ever came along to shake my memory of him. I'm so thankful today; something I never thought God would grant to me is real love and caring from a guy.

August 16, The rain is really coming down and do we ever need it. The house is cooling down and I love it. Ick likes it to; she crawled right up by the window to feel the cool breeze. Time is going so fast. Each day races by because I am so happy to be with Lyle. Life with him is not long enough. I love him so.

Lyle planned an early honeymoon. We went to Hayward, Wisconsin and stayed overnight. I asked a service station attendant to make coffee even though it was late in the evening. Lyle was not happy with me. She did make the coffee and I drank it. The next day we went on to Duluth, Minnesota. I had never been to Northern Wisconsin or Minnesota in all the years that I lived back there. This was a wonderful trip. We saw so much beauty and it was fun because we shared it with each other.

We put up more hay. I don't remember if it was second or third crop. Haying is something that I always enjoyed doing and it was a lot of fun helping Lyle. We also spent time visiting his family, Mom, my son, daughter, and their families.

I saved notes that Lyle wrote for me when I was at his place: "you are loved by the world's luckiest man "

"you are the ideal woman so easy to love"

"Grace is easy to love, so full of life, and so nice to be with. No pen can write the love I feel for her. I must pray every day to be worthy of her love."

And as I write this story, I am overwhelmed with the knowledge of how much Lyle loved me. I am so grateful for his love, and I pray that I made his life better.

September 4 Journal; this is such a beautiful time of the year; the nights are cool and the days just right. The big yellow moon is full and hangs just above the horizon giving us it's beauty to share. Soon I'll be leaving for Spokane and my heart feels heavy and sad. I love Lyle so deeply; the touch of his hand; the closeness we feel; the warmth from his eyes, his smile, and his reassuring words.

We will be back to letters and the distance that allows no touch.

Days and nights will become eternity's that will finally end this winter and hopefully forever if that is the Lords will. I will miss him so and pray that all will be well for him; that God will watch over and protect him for all of his days on this earth.

Lyle is delivering mail today. I miss his presence a lot because of the time we are going to have to be apart that's soon to come. We went to pick hazelnuts yesterday but the squirrels and chipmunks beat us to them. Maybe this is going to be the real tough winter they are predicting due to the Mexican volcano. The sun is almost high enough to start warming the earth. The nights leave heavy dew now and the sun is losing its warmth. Another year proceeds onward as time slows for no one.

BACK IN COLLEGE

MY LAST QUARTER apart from Lyle. As I and Amber were putting all of Lyle's and my letters in notebooks according to dates, I came across this and had to laugh out loud! I bet Lyle almost fell off his chair laughing when he got this so-called drawing of a Neuron and all that went with it!

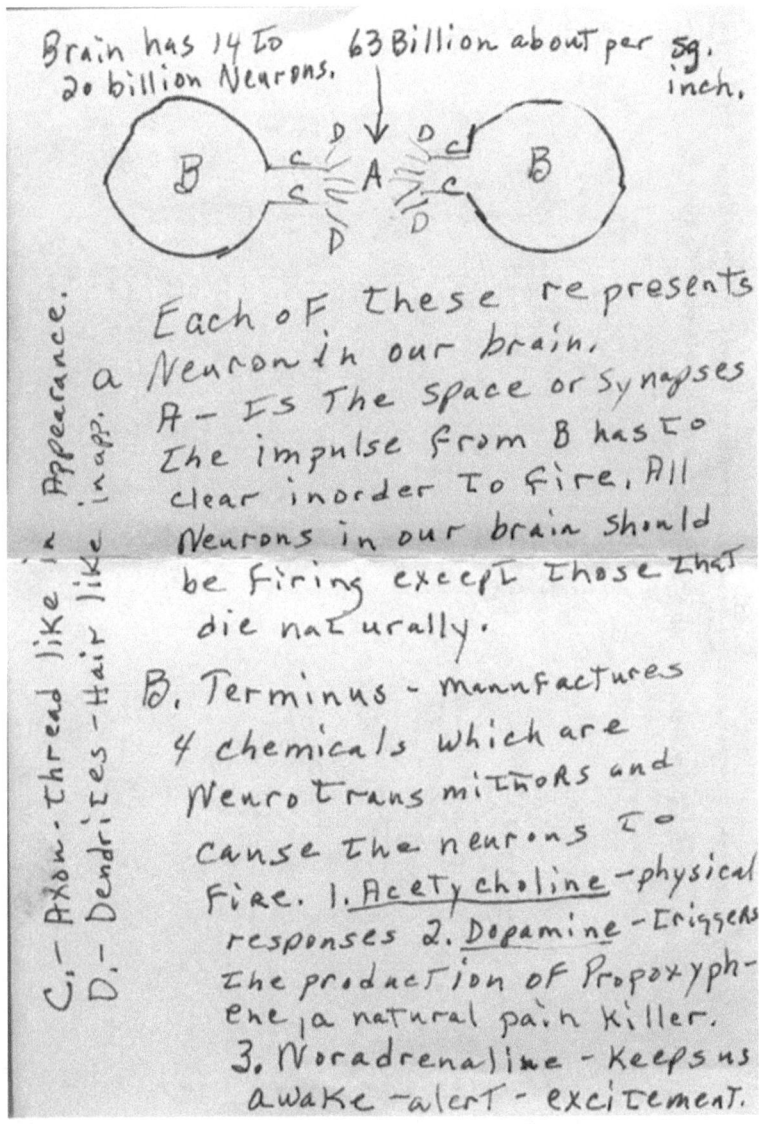

Note the grease spot on the corner from Lyle's fingers. Bet he's still laughing.

4. Serotinin - Our emotions.

50% of Marijuana is still in the body after 7 days still causing an adverse affect on neurons.

Acetaldehyde from Liquor also stays for days or months + causes damage to our neurons.

LSD will replace the chemicals in the Terminus and cause a Flashback. A flashback after 1 yr. is doubtful.

Neurons die;
 1. Naturally beginning at about age 12.
 2. Any fever over 102.
 3. A bump on the head hard enough to hurt.
 4. Drugs - Especially Alcohol + Cocaine.

Knowing this - Guess thats why as many billion neurons!

It seems extreme that some people can drink in drugs enough to thin a 2 Billion neurons and become Wet Brains.

MORE LETTERS FROM LYLE

SEPTEMBER 24, 1982: "It is only Friday; a week ago we were talking about how to get the meat back with you."

Note: I wanted to put it in a card board box and Lyle would not hear of his fiancée getting on an airplane with a cardboard box! I don't recall what we put it in but the meat made it to Spokane without thawing.

24th cont: "today was a cool day; I trucked corn to Durand then cut some logs for wood. I can't find a copy of the song you wrote for me; must've worn it out carrying it around showing it to people. I don't feel very cheerful; missing you too much. Today I got two letters from you."

"First the 18-month winter I was telling you about that happened in the 1800's. It was caused by the volcanic explosion in the East Indies called Krakatoa. If we ever get to our wilderness home, we will have to get a goat; much easier to milk than a cow and just the right amount of milk too."

Note: Lyle forgot that he hates goats. And when we had orphan foals in later years, we would get goats milk from the neighbors. I don't know how many times Lyle took a swig of goat's milk out of the gallon jug we kept in the refrigerator with our milk, and too late found out it was goat's milk; he didn't like the taste at all.

24th cont: "Nora calls me last night; she wanted a marking harness for her sheep buck. She had borrowed one last year and lost it. Her house is not done yet. It is 44 x 32 so that is going to be some home, and a two-story at that. The leaves are turning and in a few days, they will be in their glory. I don't know of any place that I would rather be right now. Today will be a week that we have been apart; just a few more to go and we will be together again. I love you. Bye love and all that silly stuff."

September 27: "A big day at the mailbox. Two letters from you and a card from Cindy. Boy you are really hot to get me out there and working; what happened to the girl who was willing to make a living for both of us. I was looking forward to lying around reading and watching TV. Your letter of the 23rd; Butternuts look a lot like walnuts only they are egg shaped. Why are you bringing up trees? Do you want to lose another battle after the one we had over Tamarack trees and finding that you were wrong all along? That should be enough for you."

Note: Lyle said the trees we have in Montana are Larch. I had always heard them called Tamarack. On our Honeymoon Trip he showed me true Tamarack. I still didn't believe him until he showed me the facts in his tree book.

September 27 cont: "I have a roast in now and I will take a bath as it is warm in here; I'm getting pretty sleepy. I sent National Geographic a change of address. When you go to the post office tell them to look for it; they are supposed to deliver mail by box number but who knows. I will take a load of corn to Durand and get a haircut. Hang tight and don't blow away. I will get there and stay so long that you will be glad to see me go. Lots of love and kisses and hugs."

September 28: "At last some excitement; I took the corn to Durand. I pulled the knob to raise the box then got out of the truck; the box kept going up then the stakes broke, and the back of the box blew off. 200 bushel of corn six inches deep covers a pretty big area. It took a lot of shoveling and sweeping to get it all cleaned up. I stopped at the lumber yard and picked up 4 two by fours then stopped at Bernard's to rebuild it. I found some paint so I repainted the whole box; not the best job as it was very windy. I even got some paint in my hair more than a little in fact; now I'm a redhead. I will get that haircut tomorrow. I didn't get home until six, got the mail, and have one letter from you. I loaded corn in the dark until the moon came up; it's about 7/8 full. I think this will be the harvest moon. The wind is very strong tonight with little clouds that keep passing in front of the moon; It's like turning a light off and on. Lots of leaves are blowing around; a real spooky night but warm. For an ex-logger you surely don't know much about trees or nuts either. I am going to try to tell you what kind of trees you have by your telling me about the leaves. The Farmer's Almanac is predicting a warm winter. Oh hell, I can't sleep; probably because I'm hungry. The roast was a poor one; all bones and fat. I gave the kitties some and they growled at each other. It's the first time they have had meat."

"Here are some of the things that I have done that I think I could do again to someone's satisfaction. Concrete finishing, concrete form work, heavy equipment; dozers, front end loaders, prime loaders, etc., fork lifts, trucks of all types and sizes, building like hammer and saw etc., blasting in quarries or mines, tying rebar, all types of farm work (yuck), machine repair, or assembly. I was also a deck hand on a tow boat. I'm also a good hand with a chainsaw, have operated a jackhammer, and I don't mind heights."

October 4: "Today was a day when I really wish that you were here. The auctioneer was here and I'm kind of leaning towards having the auction this fall; about the 20th. I'm just getting tired of trying to make a decision; so much for that. I stopped at Dean's Saturday after work. Old Pappy told me what a swell girl that you were. Then Dean's wife started crying and says she will be visiting us in Spokane. Everyone got a free phone book so I delivered 380 phonebooks today; they filled my backseat. Now I have a flat tire and when I get the route done my car will have over 100,000 miles on it. I sold some corn Friday and he paid me tonight so here is the ring money and enough to buy some T-shirts for me. I am kind of restless tonight and probably won't sleep too well. I don't know why you want to get my letters; I can't write near as well as you can. It's Tuesday morning and not much sleep last night; just lying there thinking of all the things that could go wrong at the auction. Now this a.m. the stove is out of gas. Must get going and get things done; too many things to do and not much time. I love you and need you and will be by your side. Will write to you tonight."

October 8: "I wrote you a letter last night then tore it up this morning; too many misspelled words. I put the sawmill on the auction but will want a good price for it. Auctions take a lot of time and preparation. Bowser spends a lot of time at Lloyd's; he's trapping gophers. Bowser eats them. Spike found that they are too much for him; they bite back. The rain quit but the wind is pretty strong. I had maple nut ice cream and bananas for supper. I wish you were here so I would have someone to lean on. I don't know what to write you. Love and sweet words."

October 5: "today is a long gray day and my mood matches. The tractor won't start and my pickups being fixed. Bernard's pickup has a flat tire and needs 4 new ones. Fixing the pickup will cost about $300 but it will be good for quite a few more miles. My back hurts like it is broken; It must be my kidneys maybe I have a cold. I think it is because my belly sticks out and pulls my shirt up so my back gets cold. I can't get my pants up high enough to cover my back so I am getting paranoid about this belly of mine. I got three letters from you today. Nothing ever happens here. This morning it's cold and wet so I may as well clean the barn. TV said that we have 87 hours of clouds and 29 hours of rain. Sometime today I have to change a tire and get to town. I need cat food and sugar. Oh, my sheep got out yesterday and I just remembered it; I better get going."

October 8: "Bowser and I took a long walk in the woods just killing time. I walked up to Lloyd's and Ick came along. Her and Spike didn't get along so she waited outside for me and then walked home with me. Spike doesn't go out much now that it snowed; In fact, he has to be pushed out to pee. I have a soup bone on with some vegetables that taste good, but I have enough for 10 people so will have to give some to Bowser. The weather is not good for soybean harvest but there's still hope until the snow gets deep. I wish I was done and gone. I worry about you and love you and would have no future without you so please don't take any chances."

October 11: "it rained most all day yesterday and the drizzle still hasn't stopped. I fixed my TV late yesterday and just turned it off. Marty Robbins made it into the country Hall of Fame. I wish I'd been more awake when you called. I hadn't slept very well the night before and that is why I fixed the TV; if I can't sleep, I watch it and fall asleep. Eddie Rabbit is singing "I Love The Rainy Night." I'd like to put him outside here for a night or two; he would think dry. Steve came today and helped me clean the barn. He doesn't think his grades will be good enough for him to be a pilot, so he will go for a straight-line officer, and be out in 3 years. Love and hugs."

October 14th typed on the back of his auction bill: "Got 3 letters from you today; love the photo of you and Robin; one of the best of you ever. UPS brought this auction bill today.

I thought if I wrote on it, we'd have it for a souvenir. My phone is out and if I go up to Lloyd's I will have to walk as the car has a flat. It's a good thing we didn't have a flat on our honeymoon trip. I may let the mail job go rather than fix the car up again. Guess what? That cow that you said was baron had a calf. Maybe you better stay with sheep. I got the sheep in this evening. Bowser wouldn't come along because I had a gun but she got in the way when I brought them home. It's a good thing I don't have a temper or I would have shot her. The phone is working again so I will call the trucker and ship the steers. I got to go now; I wasn't going to write but I liked that picture so much that I thought I would tell you. Also, your letters aren't as kissy as they used to be what is wrong? Love and kisses."

October 19: "I borrowed Bernard's pickup as I am out of wheels today. I got to the doctor's office at 9 and it was 5 to 12 before the nurse took my blood pressure. My blood pressure is not too good; the bottom is still 100. The doctor doubled my pills and I have to go back in two weeks. He asked about my ulcer; when I told him that I didn't take the Tagament regularly he told me that ulcer would kill me faster than the blood pressure ever would. So, I will get hot on taking those pills."

"When I got home it started to rain by the bucket full then I saw that my cows were out, and had gotten into the corn crib. It looks like they have a lot of corn on the ground. I tried to chase them but they ran behind the barn. I had to race Fuzzy to the gate on the other side of the barn; that did it for her; she will be sold. I can't shut the gate in back of the barn as my nephew was driving the crawler yesterday and the track came off, so I jammed Bernard's pickup on one side and tied the gate to the crawler on the other. God, will I be glad to get out of here."

"It is still raining. I don't think I will get much sleep tonight, I'm as jumpy as a cat in a room full of rocking chairs. I can't seem to lose that big belly that I have grown this summer. Maybe it is best if we have a small wedding as you may want to hide me. Maybe the ulcer has something to do with that. I am very glad that you got your ring and I would be happier still if I could see it on your finger. It isn't too long now. I will be leaving November 29 at the earliest. I am really missing you tonight. I think I will eat one more apple. Boy it will be nice to have a smart wife; wisdom is better than riches. I hope that you're counseling works out well for you. It would be nice if you could be wrong at times. I won't fight you when you are wrong; just let you go your old pigheaded way. Well, whatever, I may as well close now and will call you Friday night late."

October 20: "I went to bed at midnight and woke up at 2:30; it is now 5:30 and I am up and dressed. It is snowing out. I wish I had a cup of coffee but I don't even have any tea so I am drinking hot lemonade; not too good. I have let Ick in again and gave her the last of the milk. Radio says the wind is 41 mph, and today is the day that we've got to get the machinery lined up for the auction. The high today will be 40 with snow flurries. So looks like I'm going to have fun in the freezing mud."

October 27: "it has been a busy week. I have been helping Bernard fill silo for other people. I work mornings and Bernard afternoons. Sunday was a warm lazy day. Bernard filled silo for the Fishers. I took his tractor home then took his pickup to the dump and Becky came along. We drove some back roads and stopped at the cemetery where my great-grandparents are buried; grandparents on Dad's side. Then we drove through the watermelon patch; lots of fun mushing the melons up."

November 1: "Nora called and asked if she could come up. I asked her if she had been drinking and why was she swearing so much. That got her mad and she never asked again.

Monday, I got going early; chopped silage till noon then went to Ellsworth. I borrowed Bernard's baler and baled the wheat straw in the afternoon. Today I worked till 2 then it started to rain so we quit. I came home and got the B ready for winter and put the haybine in the shed. I am very tired and need to get to bed. I just hate writing letters but got my phone bill today for one call was $13. Thank you for loving me; today is one day closer till I can hold you and kiss you. With all my love. All I need is you."

November 2: "Election Day at last now one can listen to the radio again. It is snowing and I am waiting for water to boil for spaghetti. I will eat then go to the doctor. I got new tires for the pickup yesterday so I dare to drive a little faster. Today is our last nice day for a while as a cold front is coming in. 6 PM and I'm back from the doctor. My blood pressure is just right but he wants to see me 1 more time; he will give me my records to take along. The nurse weighed me; too much the most that I've ever weighed. The doctor says fruits and low- fat meat, and it's better to have a big tum than black lungs. I think that I coughed up blood last weekend but forgot to ask the doctor about that. I forgot to vote so I better get going."

November 3: "it's still snowing but not very hard. Nora is on the phone talking about her house; boring. Now she is telling me what a great looking guy Lloyd is; trying to make me jealous, I guess.

Thank God she hung up. I don't have a lot to write about. I do miss you more each day and I want you to talk to, to ask you what you think about things. Did I tell you that John and Sandy's big red dog got killed? They never had a dog in all the years they've been married then they got to liking Bowser so they got Sam. Best that I go to work and cut some wood or get some straw bales around the house. I love you and I'm proud of you."

November 8: "2 letters from you today; a bright spot in an otherwise gloomy day. The combiners didn't get a thing done today, and tomorrow it's going to rain. The man that he hired to run the combine got mad and went home. If the combiners would get their act together, I would get them to combine my corn. I went to get some meat today from my freezer. There's only 10 pieces left. Thank God we rented that locker in Plum City. This evening I walked out to look for deer. I took the 22; it's a good thing I left the 30-30 at home as I got close to 8 deer. When they saw me, they ran; I shot in the air then ran after them just to see them go. But when I ran, I lost my pal Bowser; she hates guns. Ick had come along and she stayed with me." November 9: "I woke up at three this morning hungry; diets are the pits; no munchies in the house. If the rain slows up, I will cut wood. I just thought of something to do; I will balance my checkbook that will pass the day. Now that I have something to do I think I will get to work. I love you very much; You are my one true love; The one worth waiting for. We will be together in a matter of weeks weather permitting. Love and hugs."

November 10: "I am waiting for the station to call to let me know my pickup is done. Bernard will take me to get mine and leave his. Yesterday Bowser and I went for a long walk; all we got was very wet as we were gone for three hours, and it rained most of the time. We saw a lot of ducks flying north. At least I slept well last night. Oh, I noticed that I can go farther without losing my breath; maybe I will take up jogging. If I get my pick up back today, I am going to get some more boxes so I can keep on packing. It looks like it will be later than we planned although I did call and ordered the phone to be taken out November 30, so at least that is a start."

"Tomorrow is Veterans Day so no use trying to finish this letter; may as well make it a long one: you may get it Saturday with luck."

November 12: "40 mile an hour winds and a half inch of snow on the ground, and it's getting colder. This has been the worst two weeks that I can remember. The weather is so rotten that I can't get anything done although I did do some more packing this morning.

It is now noon and I haven't been outside yet. Better get this mailed; that means I will have to put my shoes on. I hope I get a letter from you today."

November 18: "Another busy day; the third day in a row that I have trucked corn for Bernard. The frost went out last night so the fields are very muddy. When I woke up Monday morning my first thought was why not get on Interstate 90 and go; why stick around here. I must've been dreaming of you just before I awoke. The last three days have been really nice; today it will get up to 50 but it may rain tomorrow. Something went wrong with the hot water heater and I don't think that I will fix it. I am supposed to work all next week. I have a low-grade cold that I hope will not get any worse, but delivering mail with the window open won't help. If we just get a nice week, I can wrap things up here pretty good and be by your side soon."

"I was having a sandwich at Bernard's today at noon. Becky was feeling really low as she has been working hard and there's been a lot of school doings too. She was telling me how bad her headache was and I told her all she needed was someone to hold her for a few minutes and tell her that things will be better soon; she said that I was right. (how about that) It is too bad that Bernard isn't more demonstrative; it would make life a lot easier for them. I think most people take each other for granted and forget to reassure one another. I went to Plum City and Becky came and got me. My truck didn't run right like the gas wasn't flowing right. Can't think of anything worth the labor of writing. Next week will be the last full week that I will be here with luck."

November 25: "Happy Thanksgiving. I started combining today. It started snowing like it was going to make up for lost time; the last trip down that steep hill was a real thrill. I slipped and fell in the snow tonight. Bowser thought that was the greatest thing; she ran a big circle and then tried to sit on my lap. Ick came along and got rolled in the snow a few times. I think Ick has moved in for the winter; she was making such pretty little tracks until the dog rolled her over. My sister Alice just called. She will type up addresses for us. She thinks that I should get going because you might get tired of waiting. I told her that I am worth waiting for. It's like I told Becky that you are never going to meet another ME."

"I'm sending you Bowser's rabies vaccine certificate. I thought it might be nice to have in case she bites someone. I got the phone bill yesterday, almost $70 and that is just October. If I don't call it isn't because I don't love you; It's because I need the money for the trip to Spokane."

November 27: "Today was my last day at the post office. I am getting tired of all these last things but they are necessary if I am to have my first day as your husband; it can't come soon enough for me. I have to go to the doctor Monday although I feel good. I may have gained some more weight though. Did the dishes; I thought about going to town but same old beer and deer stories. I guess I will find something to read."

November 29: "I went to the doctor today. My blood pressure isn't as good as it should be. We had a long talk; he wants me to walk for a half hour a day then he wants you to check my blood pressure often to see what the averages are. My pulse should be 50 if I rest for at least 10 minutes. The doctor gave me my records to take with me. Ick is just playing all by herself racing around; she must be feeling good. Well, I better close and get some rest. I've got a deal for you; you can go with the sailor in that photo. Till I get there I will warn you that he is older and he has put on some weight. Darling if things go right, I will soon be there. Oh boy, no more damn letters or large phone bills. I love you the most."

December 1: "I took the phone out this morning and I miss it already. At least Nora will leave me alone now. We had thunderstorms last night; some December. Alice was here today and gave me the addresses. She found a card that you had sent to Mother and Dad years ago. It was signed Mrs. Grace Bach and family. Boy, you had a lot better handwriting then. It was a nice card too; a Hallmark. It must've been from Montana as it has a weather report enclosed. I woke up sometime last night thinking that my heart had stopped. I must have been thinking about those pills the doctor gave me. I told Alice about it and she said that is the best death that one could ask for; as a nurse she has seen a lot of bad deaths."

December 3: "Well you ruined this letter by calling so it will be short. I have said goodbye to some people three times; I need to get going. I don't have anything to write about today. By the way is our romance so dull that you think I need a weather report when you call? I won't stay here if I think the weather out there is bad so don't worry. The moon is shining bright tonight and a nice breeze is blowing. Maybe it will dry out the fields. I bet by now you have already looked into flying here and riding with me to Spokane. Bet we wander all over the West on the way as you show me off. I love you and you only. Without you near there is no tomorrow;

see you soon. December 9: "With luck this will be my last letter to you for a long time. We should have a good trip back as the pickup is running like never before. Do you think the Black Hills would still be open? I thought that maybe we may as well have another honeymoon although life with you will be one long honeymoon. I better close now as you may not get this before you leave. Grace said that we could stay with her and Lloyd when you get back here but I don't want to welcome you to someone else's home. We will stay at my place even though everything is packed up and ready to go.

My December 9 letter to Lyle: "You don't know it yet but I will be there the 13th at 8:59 PM on Western's flight 412 via Salt Lake. I am so happy and walking on air. How am I going to study for my 2 finals Monday? My plane leaves Monday afternoon. Marty Robbins died. I am so glad for his music especially, "Old Memories Never Die." Darling, I Love You."

LEAVING THE FARM

IT WAS VERY cold as we packed and loaded his pickup. A snow storm was brewing when we left. We took I-90 on our trip to Spokane. By the time we got to Jackson, MN the freeway was closed; to us that was an adventure. We were still young enough at heart that weather and bad roads were a challenge.

Our next stop was Livingston, Montana. We rented a motel room then parked the pickup in the garage next to our unit. Surprise, Surprise, we couldn't get the doors open wide enough to exit the pickup. Lyle backed out and parked on the street.

We ate supper at a restaurant then had a drink at the bar. A mural of the beautiful mountains of Glacier Park were on the wall behind the bar. I told Lyle those were of Glacier Park's mountains. He said they weren't; they had to be Alaskan or Canadian mountains. When he finally saw the mountains in Glacier I was proven right. I don't think he admitted it and I didn't say, "I told you so."

Our trip was uneventful except for the dog and cat. Ick started to get out of the box and Bowser felt she belonged in that box. As soon as Ick stuck her head out Bowser promptly snapped at her, and put a big paw on her head pushing her back into the box. Both the cat and dog did make the trip very well in spite of this. We would get out and stretch our legs and let them out so they could stretch theirs. Ick found a dead bird and pretended like she had stalked and caught it all on her own.

Our next night was spent in Ronan, MT. My family lived near Ronan and Polson, and I wanted them to meet Lyle. Several years later we decided to stay in that same motel in Ronan. The bed looked fine until I sat on the edge. We discovered that the bed had been broken and propped up. That sure cooled our memories of that nice motel. As the years went on, we found out just how good we were at finding the worst motels!

Like the time in South Dakota Lyle raced a man to the desk and lost; we had to drive another 100 miles to a motel. Another time we thought we'd found the very last motel. When we woke up and looked out the window it was about 50 feet straight down into a canyon, and we passed at least 5 motels when we left that morning.

Then there was the time we were sight-seeing in the Custer, SD area. We'd gone into the back country quite a way when we found a vacant old shack that we decided to investigate. The hair stood up on our necks when we opened the refrigerator and it was on with food inside! We got away from there in a hurry. By the time we got back to civilization all the motels but one was full. We named the one we stayed in the "covered wagon" motel. The bed was a piece of plywood with a very thin mattress. A black and white 12-inch TV sat on a dusty, wooden ledge in one corner. We did not have a restful night's sleep.

Years later in 2010 we took a trip down to Yellowstone Park with Lyle's nephew and his wife. They went on to Colorado and we drove to Cody to visit a close friend. I had made reservations on line before we left because I knew Cody motels were always full during the summer. We pulled into our reserved motel which looked pretty trashy. The inside was awful; yellow walls, a yellowing tub, very worn, frayed carpet that hadn't been cleaned in years. The bed was a single mattress and so uncomfortable. We didn't bother to use the tub or sink, but got dressed and washed up in the rest room of the cafe where we met our friend for breakfast.

SPOKANE

BACK TO OUR trip to Spokane; we arrived in Spokane 10 days before our wedding. Robin and Dan had the tree up and decorated. They were glad to see us arrive safely. Jean was all excited and we started planning for our wedding with enthusiasm. Lyle wasn't used to driving in big cities and Spokane was not only big; it was built on hills. He soon found his way around. As we planned for our wedding time went by in a flash. We had a rehearsal several days ahead of time. The day of our wedding I was getting my hair styled. Lyle had gone with me and was talking to the beautician. His warm conversation with her awakened my green-eyed monster. His voice was always so special, and it was supposed to be for me only.

Lyle always listened to the person he was communicating with; another of his special traits.

I wrote a love letter to Lyle the day before our wedding: "Dearest Darling, I want you to know that I'm so happy with you and I'm proud to become your wife. In my wildest dreams this was never a reality. Yes, a fantasy but I was so sure you wouldn't love me, and also that you were probably already married. Thank you, Darling, for making me so happy. This past week has been very pleasant and comfortable for me. All the days I've had with you went by like a flash because I have enjoyed them so much. My only regret for my marriage to you is our life will go by too fast because to be with you is to enjoy every day, and to really live. I'm so glad you have asked me to be your woman and your wife to share the joy, the bad, the good, and the sad. Always I will use kind words when speaking to you and treat you with the highest respect, and give you all the love I have to give for as long as God's willing to let me be. With all my love, Grace

We made up our wedding vows:

Lyle's: "As I am now, I will always be the same person that you love today."

Mine were a little more elaborate: "I, Grace, promise to love you, Lyle, with all of my heart and soul. I will give your life joy and meaning by sharing all of the good and do my best to soften any storms. I pray that I will put as much sunshine into your life as you have put into mine."

OUR SONG

WHEN I WAS 12 years old I heard Russ's Song. I remembered this song when planning our wedding 30 years later. I wanted it sang at our wedding for Lyle to let him know how much I loved him. It's as if this song was written just for him! It fits his warmth, his soft heart, and the depth of his character. I had to go to several music stores before I found the sheet music for this song.

On our anniversaries we would listen to the tape of our wedding songs and light our candle. When Russ's Song would play, I would shed tears of thankfulness for my husband.

Russ's Song

I thought I'd write a song for you
it's just to say I care
The nights are often dreams of you
and my days are filled with prayer

I sometimes wish that you could see
my heart for just a day
I'd wonder what you'd think and do
and even what you'd say

Our lives belong to Jesus
and we know He comes first

But sometimes when I'm farthest down
and things are looking worst
I see your warm brown eyes
and the tears begin to fall

God knew just who I needed
and He's with me after all
Don't think you're on a pedestal
I know the bad things too

But what I see and what I love
is Jesus using you
The gentleness of spirit
and the understanding heart
The tender smile that comforts me
they're all the Jesus parts

And so you see you strengthen me
your love is used of Him
To bless me when I need it most
and when the way looks dim
I don't expect you'll understand
just why its you I love
I only hope I brought to you (this was "bring to you")
some blessings from above

OUR WEDDING

We were married in a friend's home on December 30, 1982. A wonderful young woman sang our wedding songs beginning with Russ's Song. We chose "How Great Thou Are", "Endless Love", "You Light Up My Life", and "Whither Thou Goest I Will Go." My son and daughter, my uncle, Fred and his wife, Ann, along with many of my close friends from college attended. We were married by a minister. This honeymoon was 1 night in a motel in Coeur d'Alene, Idaho.

We celebrated Lyle's 47th birthday at home January 1, 1983 with a nice dinner, and a birthday cake. For years I made a Chocolate Mallow Cake for his birthday; that had to stop when we both gained way too much weight.

December 30, 1982 8:30 PM

ANOTHER DREAM

AFTER LYLE'S DEATH I yearned for a dream with him in it; after 8 months I got my wish. Someone was trying to wrestle me to the ground to rob or kill me; all at once Lyle came driving up in the pickup. I was saved. I awoke immediately and was so happy that he had appeared in a dream.

We were always excited to see each other at the end of our work days or if one of us went someplace. Each other's presence would brighten our arrival home. After Lyle was unable to get out to do chores, I always looked at the lighted window knowing he was waiting for me to return from the barn. Frequently my hands would be ice cold; his hands were always warm until the last weeks of his life. He would hold my cold hands in his to warm them. But as his health failed his hands became so cold my hands would actually warm his. I asked Lyle why he had never married. He said, "I stayed single because I measured every woman, I met against you." This continued during our marriage too. He would observe women in stores, etc. and state how they didn't measure up to me. What a wonderful and lasting memory of my husband's love.

Throughout our years together Lyle always referred to me as "his bride" when speaking to friends. During his last days with me he would tell me how beautiful he thought I was. For that I am thankful because I never considered myself even pretty much less beautiful.

It is now almost 2 years since Lyle's death. My emotions are thawing; it seemed I was sailing through all of this but the grief has hit big time. I am so thankful for the years we had and especially that Lyle was not alone when he died. I was right there with him, at his side in seconds after hearing him fall. Had my first dream not happened we would never have known our wonderful love, and Lyle may have died alone. My heart aches at the very thought.

The last weeks before his death Lyle had been grieving over the years we were not together; all 18 of them. I thought I had done this grief work when we were first married but it is creeping in again along with the tears. I visualize him handsome, young, strong, and everything I ever wanted, and wishing we had been together from childhood on. As we loved one another in our mid and later years how wonderful it would have been to have known and loved each other then. The very brief times we had together as young adults were special, special enough to last through the 18 years we were apart. My grandfather wanted a family member to take over the ranch; looking back I'm sure Lyle and I would have done so and loved every minute of it. Wishful reminiscing; the ranch was in Rattlesnake Gulch and lived up to the name. Had we married years ago and made our home there we'd most likely been snake bit anyway.

ENJOYING SPOKANE

IN MARCH OF '83 we went back to Wisconsin for the rest of our things from the farm. The trip was sad because Lyle was angry with me for smoking. I also reacted to his drinking with his nephew and embarrassed him in front of his family. We went to Wisconsin by way of Highway 2 stopping at my sisters on our way, and returning to Spokane by way of Interstate 90.

When we got back from Wisconsin, I started my last quarter of college. Graduation was June 9, 1983. I was able to graduate with honors, and Lyle attended my graduation. It was a beautiful time and yet very scary because now the job search became critical.

We did find time to enjoy Spokane's Manito and Riverside Parks. Manito was a photographer's dream with all the flowers. In the spring we enjoyed the tulips and budding foliage. The Lilacs were especially beautiful. Summer was a great time for a walk through the park. It was way too big to ever see everything in the time we had; 90 acres of ornate beauty. The roses on Rose Hill were in bloom before we moved to Colstrip. The Perennial Garden had every flower imaginable and the Nishinomiya Japanese Garden was unique with a beauty all of its own. We really missed this beautiful park.

Riverfront Park is a public park in downtown Spokane, Washington. It is located along the Spokane River containing the upper Spokane Falls and just upstream from the lower falls. It was created for Expo '74, a World's Fair event. The Park is well known for the Riverfront Park Carousel as well as the IMAX theatre, clock tower, and the skyride over the falls. It encompasses 100 acres.

We went to several movies at the IMAX. Lyle had been to an IMAX theatre before but it was a first for me. The Eruption of Mount St. Helens' movie was so real; it was like we were right in the middle of it. The Riverfront Park Carousel was built by Charles Looff in 1909. The carousel contains 54 horses, 1 giraffe, 1 tiger, 1 goat, and 2 chariots, all hand carved by Looff himself. It also has a ring dispenser that allows the outside riders to grab a ring during each pass and then toss the ring at a clown with a hole for his mouth.

Lyle was like a kid when we rode on the carousal. He would jump from horse to horse, hang off the side, grab the ring and toss it, and embarrassed me to no end. Lyle knew how to have fun and I didn't. Over the years he would say I reminded him of Buddy Holly's song, "You're So Square."

Our time in the parks took us away from everyday life to a place of pure beauty, wonder, and pleasure. When we moved to Eastern Montana it took time for us to appreciate the raw beauty of the dry land.

The Riverfront Carousal

We took sight-seeing trips every weekend that we could. One trip was through Kettle Falls and on into Canada. On the way home we rounded a corner on the highway when I saw this white object on the hillside. "Oh, a mountain goat," I said. As usual my brain was disengaged. It was a white horse and Lyle had a good laugh.

Speaking before my brain was in gear was common. Another time we were on our way to Billings, Montana. A sign said," Lewis And Clark Tracts. "I said," How do they know?"

My immediate reaction to the sign was "tracks" and not tracts. Again, my husband had a good laugh.

Then the time I was looking at the map trying to find LA. I said, "I can find Los Angeles but I can't find LA." Lyle never did let me forget that one.

In my defense I'd taken 2 grades at once and was through the 8th grade by the time I was 12.

High School was a correspondence course, and geography wasn't one of the subjects I chose.

I finished that course when my oldest son was 2 years old. I was 19. Another trip took us to Grand Coulee Dam, and Electric City. On the way home the gas tank started to show empty. We didn't have any cash and credit cards weren't even in our vocabulary. An older gentleman accepted our check. He said his eye sight was so bad he couldn't even tell if the check was filled out correctly, but that kind old man saved our day.

One evening we canoed Loon Lake enjoying the sounds of the birds, and watching the ducks as they swam. It was so quiet and peaceful. We wished it could have lasted forever.

Before Lyle found a steady job, he cut firewood. When a tree would fall Bowser would be gone. Once she didn't come when he was ready to go home so he left his jacket, and the next day she was laying on that jacket and glad to see him.

Lyle started working for Meidling Concrete Inc. He was putting in very long hours; many of his days would start at 4 AM and end at 9 PM. They were repairing the airstrip at the Fairchild Air Base along with several other jobs. Lyle was so exhausted when he came home and his knees were causing him tremendous pain. The only positives were his wages and he was very slim. Lyle brought home a Billings, Montana paper with an ad for a Chemical Dependency Counselor so I arranged a job interview. It was for mid-July which corresponded with my flight to my son's wedding in Minnesota. I stopped in Billings on my way home for the interview and was hired. Lyle's job, my son's wedding, and my interview were all providential. His job allowed us to have enough money to move to Colstrip. It would have been impossible for me to ever arrange such significant events within such a fine timeframe.

I was glad to get home to Lyle. We began planning our move to Colstrip; my new job began on August 15th, 1983. We had 13 days to pack and move over 700 miles, and we wanted to have at least three days to unpack when we arrived in Colstrip.

COLSTRIP

COLSTRIP; WHEN WE drove through this town in March of '83 I made the remark, "who would want to live in this godforsaken place?" And there we were because I guess God decided we could certainly live there and he wouldn't forsake us.

Lyle went to Wisconsin to visit his family in November. My daughter came home with him for Thanksgiving. She and her husband were having problems. Lyle said it snowed so bad from Belle Fourche, South Dakota to Colstrip that he could hardly see to drive. Dan and Robin came over for Thanksgiving. The holiday wasn't what we anticipated. Rene missed her husband and could talk of nothing else. Robin and Dan argued all the time. We took Rene to Billings so she could fly back to Minnesota Saturday morning. The roads were a sheet of ice and she was expecting their baby any day. Dan and Robin had left for Spokane on Friday and Rene made it to Red Wing safely on Saturday. Lyle and I needed some time to recover from the kids and their problems.

That recovery didn't last long because Dan had no more than got back to Spokane than he decided to come and live with us. We were disgusted since we had to send an Amtrak ticket to him, and Lyle had to drive 210 miles to meet him in Glasgow, MT. Our life changed a lot with Dan home again. I do not envy anyone with teenagers especially when they're also trying to build a new relationship. René had a little girl December 17, 1983. Her marriage was not to be. They had split up for good. Lyle and I went to Miles City and bought our new granddaughter a complete layette.

Our first anniversary was December 30th, and so much had happened in that year. We went to the B&R for our anniversary dinner. They baked a special cake for us. We went home, played our songs, lit our candle and exchanged wedding vows once more. We had made it one year in spite of the trials along the way.

Lyle was 48 January 1, 1984. I made him the chocolate mallow cake and gave him a belt buckle.

That spring I got the idea that we needed to buy a house instead of renting. Even though Lyle was against it, we bought an older trailer with a tip-out. "Better than paying rent was my motto." Well, that didn't last long because it rained. Lyle found me setting on the floor in my new house with water leaking into the living room like a sieve, and I was crying! He didn't say "I told you so" but he wasn't happy! It took us 3 months to get it fixed up enough to be livable. My husband had the patience of Job during that trying time.

In July of 1984 I was transferred to the Forsyth office. We were able to move our trailer to a lot closer to Forsyth by November. That meant that Lyle would have to drive 60 miles a day round trip to his job in Colstrip. He trusted his driving more than mine driving that distance in all sorts of weather.

Thanksgiving Day we went after wood and spent a wonderful day in the Custer Forest. We had so much fun getting wood. It wasn't work to us. By the time we headed towards home all the restaurants were closed. We stopped at the B&R and bought some Chinese food to prepare. Our evening was spent in warm conversation eating eggs rolls.

Lyle cut this wood when we lived in Spokane.

Doing what he loved in the Custer National Forest.

Our 2nd Anniversary was spent at home; it was just too cold to go anywhere. I made a Mandarin Beef Dinner. We played our songs, lit our candle, and exchanged vows.

The Spring Of 1985: The place where we had our trailer had room for a big garden. Lyle loved to garden and had a tremendous garden every year of our lives together.

PUTTING DOWN ROOTS

JUNE 1985: WE took our first paid vacation together. Our journey took us through South Dakota where we picked up a topper for our new 1985 Ford Ranger. We visited family while we were in Minnesota and Wisconsin. I was so proud of my handsome and wonderful husband.

July 1985, we took a trip to Spokane. It was very stressful because of my daughter's drug use. We left Spokane tired and arrived home a lot more tired. I arranged for her to go to treatment. One of her friends drove her to our place and Lyle took her to treatment in Glasgow, a round trip of 425 miles. A lot of good that did; she left treatment after 10 days.

Fall of 1985: I went to treatment for my cigarette addiction. Treatment lasted 10 days and I couldn't wait to get home to Lyle. I had taken the train from Glasgow to Yakima and back. Amtrak was late getting into Glasgow. On my way home I took the cut off road from Flowing Springs to Rock Springs, Montana. That saves 40 miles but it is impassable when muddy. I was in such a hurry to get home I took the cut off anyway. The Monte Carlo made it through but it was challenging, and scary. There aren't any homes for miles in that area of Montana. I was wearing a yellow dress and my foot wear were sandals. I could just see me walking! The car was low on gas because of the effort it took to drive through abysmal mud. Thankfully, a well driller who lived near Rock Springs happened to be home, and he had some gas!

By the time I made it to Miles City I hadn't eaten for over 9 hours. My head was spacey and I wasn't sure I'd be able to drive home, but after eating I felt better. Grocery shopping took more time, and the car needed gas. But I made it home a half hour before Lyle came home from work. It was wonderful to be home with the love of my life.

October 1985: Each evening I would walk at least 2 miles to meet Lyle as he was coming home from work; he didn't get off work until 11 PM. A scary night put a stop to that. Lyle had warned me not to be out walking along the highway after dark. I'm sure he was more concerned about traffic. I had gotten as far as our mail box braving fears of rattlesnakes and skunks never thinking about coyotes. All at once coyote howls started and it didn't sound like 1 lone coyote. The hair stood up on the back of my neck and I was scared to death. My prayers were answered when a big, white dog came up to me; he was either a Maremma or Great Pyrenees. He would walk ahead of me for a while then come back to my side. He stayed with me the half mile to the bridge, that was close to the house, then he turned and vanished as he had come like a ghost in the night. Years later we found out he belonged to a neighbor, and he had been shot. We both felt sad when we heard about his death.

We hauled firewood Lyle had cut the 12th, 13th, 19th, and 26th of October. A cold rain dampened our spirits some on the 12th but Lyle built a fire, and we warmed up as we ate lunch. The other days were beautiful although warm. We could see the beautiful Big Horn Mountains in the distance. They were at least 60 miles from us but the snowcapped peaks seemed to bring them closer.

The 19th was warm; we were both sweating as we cut and loaded firewood. We were wishing we'd picked a cooler day. We drove home by way of Ashland and had a flat tire right by the 212 Diner. Fortunately, we didn't have to unload too much wood before Lyle was able to jack the trailer up. He had just slipped the spare on when the jack gave out.

That summer we camped in the Big Horns by Sucker Creek several times. We saw does with their fawns, the most beautiful buck, and even a moose.

We had also taken a trip into Canada that summer. The Radium Hot Springs area was beautiful but the Custer National Forest and the Big Horn Mountains were every bit as nice.

When we moved to Rosebud County we hadn't planned to stay. We even thought seriously of moving to Wisconsin. As the years went by we began to appreciate the beauty of the area, and we had good jobs.

November 2nd was a warm day. We had gone to the Custer Forest by way of O'Dell Creek then on up to the Poker Jim Lookout. From the Lookout one can see for hundreds of miles in all directions. On our way home we saw several deer. Our trip home with this load of wood was uneventful.

November 9, 1985: Winter arrived with high winds and snow falling throughout the day. Our wood stove sure felt good. Lyle was reading a Wambaugh book and I was answering letters; this was way before email. "Fred" our cat went outside just long enough to go potty. We named her Fred after her spaying. The hearth was her favorite wintertime place. Ick had died when we lived in Colstrip, and Lyle had taken Bowser back to his brother's farm in Wisconsin. We hauled another load of wood from the Custer Forest on the 16th. Lyle had cut down a huge Pine tree. We had hoped to go back for several more loads but winter came in for good.

CHANGES

1986 BROUGHT QUITE a few changes. My sister's father died October 1st. I was glad I could be with her at his funeral in Terry, Montana. Debs was in my life for 6 years; his leaving in 1948 was painful for my sister and I.

My ex and his wife divorced. Lyle's brother, Lloyd, passed away November 14th. Lyle left for Wisconsin the 15th. We had been in Wisconsin that summer so Lyle had a nice visit with his brother. Sadly, he had been planning on a trip to visit Lloyd that December. He stocked up the wood and kindling before he left. I missed him and could hardly wait for him to come home.

Lyle had only been home a few days when my son called and told us he had Type 1 Diabetes. He was seriously ill requiring hospitalization in Intensive Care. That ended his Navy career and left him lost and confused for quite a while. After he was fitted with an Insulin Pump his life was a lot better, and he was able to get a very good job.

We spent our 4th Anniversary at home. For our 3rd, we had gone to the Long Branch in Rosebud for dinner. The meal was poor with the steak rare; we both liked our meat well done. So, spending our 4th at home wasn't so bad. We enjoyed cube steaks, baked potatoes, and salad. This anniversary, as always, ended with our songs, lighting our candle, and exchanging our vows.

For Lyle's birthdays we always had that fabulous Chocolate Mallow Cake.

1987:

Robin was back into drugs again if she was ever off them; we didn't know for sure if she'd ever stopped using. As a child she was so energetic and full of life. Years later I found out a female teacher had been molesting her. This seems to have set the pattern of self-destruction through-out her life. Robin passed away from multiple sclerosis in 2006 after leading an emotionally hectic life. She was 41 years old.

My father died February 25th. I had only seen him a few times in my life and couldn't decide on attending his funeral. I called Lyle as soon as I saw his name in the obituaries. Thank God for my kind and loving husband. In the end I decided not to go to his funeral. He had a widow and 3 grown sons who would be there. Why should I be that little girl looking in the window at a family that was never mine. My husband was the family I needed that day.

We took another summer vacation trip to Minnesota and Wisconsin. We enjoyed our 2 grandchildren and both of our families.

THE BIG RED DOG

WE HAD A phone call from my son; this was before he was diagnosed with Type 1 Diabetes.

He was going out to sea and his big red Golden Retriever was on a plane heading for Billings. Would one of us pick him up and care for him? With the dog already in the air how could we say, "No." We hadn't planned on a dog but we had one.

Lyle took Gunner to the woods. He was a City Dog, and he'd never seen a forest before. His first reaction was fear. He would look, bark, and back up. Gunner was so bewildered when he saw all those trees.

Gunner would not mind at all, and he also upset Fred Cat because he'd be tromping along when she was trying to be quiet enough to catch a mouse. The first year Lyle had chickens Gunner killed one. Lyle tied the dead chicken around his neck and made him wear that hen for quite a while. That did cure him of killing chickens, but it didn't prevent him from killing a baby turkey when we were riding up in the mountains. We hollered but too late, and he probably wouldn't have listened anyway.

Lyle rescued him from traps, pulled porcupine quills from his mouth and nose, and deskunked him. Gunner liked to lay in Lyle's tomato patch because it was nice and cool. Each time he would be reprimanded but he never did give up on the tomato patch.

Gunner loved to chase cats. When we went to visit my uncle, he chased his wife's cat up a tree upsetting Ann. We took a mare to a ranch for training. Gunner treed their cat! He didn't stop with cats either. He would dare coyotes by running through the pasture after them. Even when he was so old, he could hardly get around he'd challenge coyotes.

We had stopped at a service station to buy cold drinks when the owner asked if our dog needed water. He asked Lyle to bring the dog over to a bowl of water. The man had a dog and Gunner beat his dog up right in the middle of the highway!

We had taken a camping trip soon after Gunner arrived. He rode in the pickup camper whenever we went on a trip. When we stopped and let him out, we found a bench cushion torn to shreds. After that Gunner had to ride in his portable kennel.

When we took him to Minnesota, he dug a big hole in my daughter's back yard.

Our summers always included trips to the Big Horn Mountains. The summer of '87 found us back by Sucker Creek again. Gunner loved the water so spent a lot of time in Sucker Creek. We were awakened by a cowboy because Gunner was chasing cattle! We packed up camp and our dog. When we got down into the lowlands we stopped and let Gunner out for a run. He looked bewildered when he could only see 1 lone cow; the woods and the cattle herd were gone.

When the water would come down the canal by our place Gunner would let Lyle know. He would be so excited and went swimming many times a day throughout the summer. Gunner learned to ride in the canoe so he also canoed the Yellowstone and many smaller rivers and lakes with us.

Even with all the negatives Gunner had a special place in our hearts. He loved to go with us when we rode up into the hills, or in the Big Horn Mountains. He could keep up and usually went on ahead exploring. In the end he couldn't keep up and was so sad when we'd go and he had to stay home. Gunner was 14 when he had to be put to sleep for good. We cried.

Gunner, Meggie, and Lady sharing a granola
bar with Lyle Big Horn Mountains

EXPLORING

IN LATE SEPTEMBER we had time to explore the Red Rock Lake's area near the Montana Idaho border. We went to the Wildlife Preserve first. There we saw the Trumpeter Swans and missed seeing 3 bear and a herd of elk. From there we went on to West Yellowstone then to the Hebgen Lake area. That is where the 1959 earthquake changed the landscape. It measured 7.3 on the Richter scale and caused a huge landslide. 29 people were camping in the area, and all died. The slide blocked the flow of the Madison River resulting in the creation of Quake Lake. The 1959 quake was the strongest and deadliest earthquake to hit Montana since the 1935-36 Helena earthquakes. That one left 4 people dead. It also caused the worst landslides in the history of the Northwestern United States since 1927.

After we left the Hebgen Lake area we went west toVirginia City. The hearing for "The Mountain Men" had been held in the beautiful Virginia City Courthouse. We stopped in Ennis for gas then stayed several nights at a campground near Alder. Lyle did some fishing in the Ruby Reservoir. We found several pieces of Talc from the Talc Mine near the campground. We drove through Dillon, the Big Hole, and on to Anaconda where we visited some of my friends. I had lived in Anaconda when I worked for the Anaconda Company.

Lyle & Gunner Boot Hill near Virginia City, Montana

My uncle, Fred, and his wife, Ann, had recently moved to Phillipsburg so we stopped to see them on our way home. Ann was having a hard time getting around. Fred was feeling good and enjoyed showing us his new shop, and the log cabin he had built.

We took another trip to Helena where we toured the capitol. The murals that decorate the walls of the capitol are spectacular. This trip found us camping in the mountains between White Sulphur Springs and Townsend. The night was crisp and the moon vivid. As we walked up the trail coyotes were barking and howling. We were concerned about Gunner but he acted like he didn't even hear them. The night and all the sounds were awe-inspiring. I would like to experience that night with Lyle again forever. Being together made everything more beautiful. On our way home we went through Confederate Gulch on a mountainous dirt road. People were still mining for gold in that area. Evidence of that was all around the small creek.

When we bought the 1985 Ford, we had a topper put on it so we could take it on camping trips. The problem was unloading everything at night so we could make our bed in the back. Our load got bigger as we traveled. We stopped at a garage sale and bought a pressure cooker for $20.

Then we added souvenirs and a 50 lb sack of Idaho potatoes. We collected so much stuff it covered a picnic table, and took some time to unload each time we stopped. We looked like country bumpkins. That pressure cooker lasted through our years together and canned hundreds of quarts of fruits and vegetables. I gave it to my daughter after Lyle died.

November 1987: Lyle's chest was hurting but he was afraid to go see a doctor for fear it was lung cancer. We spent Thanksgiving in the Custer Forest getting wood. We'd forgotten our can opener and the Spam key broke so we cooked the Spam over an open fire in its container; it was delicious.

Lyle went to visit his family right after Thanksgiving. After he returned home I went to visit my family and his spending Christmas with my daughter and granddaughter. Lyle picked me up at the airport in Billings upon my return December 29th.

Our 5th Anniversary was met with snow and colder weather. We went to the new Jackpot Supper Club for dinner. Lyle had fish and I had steak. When we got home we went through our Anniversary ritual. Lyle said he'd marry me all over again. Was I ever happy to hear that?

1988: For Lyle's 52nd I made him the Chocolate Mallow Cake. Lyle asked the neighbor boy to come share with us or we'd most likely have become ill. The 2nd and 3rd of January were spent in Plentywood with my sister and her husband. They were celebrating their 25th wedding anniversary. Plentywood is as close to the North Pole as we wanted to get. It was below zero with high winds. When we stopped in Miles City on our way home it felt like a heat wave.

We took a cross country ski trip to the Big Horns and toured the Trails End Museum March 19th and 20th. We had gone to Red Lodge to cross country in February. That was a lot of fun and the trails were well groomed. I was going to show Lyle how well I could ski. I ended up upside down in a big dip in the snow. Lyle had to help me up. So much for my skill. He thought it was so funny.

Lyle Yellowstone Park 1988

    Good Friday weekend was a time for us to take trips. This time we went to Yellowstone Park.

There was very little snow so hiking was good. We had Gunner with us which is against the rules in Yellowstone. He managed to chase an antelope and that drew the attention of a park ranger. The elk were plentiful around Mammoth Hot Springs. Lyle photographed a buffalo and I was afraid he was too close. It could have been life threatening, and embarrassing if his name made the paper, especially since he grew up around livestock.

We walked over to where the Lamar River ran into the Yellowstone. Lyle took pictures of Undine Falls on Lava Creek. The Yellowstone and Lamar Rivers glistened like crystal in the sun. We walked on up to Wraith Falls which is on Lava Creek.

May of 1988, I made the decision to quit the chemical dependency facility I was working for. Lyle helped remodel an older house in Forsyth for my new office. As mentioned before the White Dove became my logo. It isn't a good idea for a workaholic to go into business for one's self! The hours I put in took so much time away from Lyle.

We made an enjoyable trip to Minnesota and Wisconsin in June with our new camper, and found nice campgrounds that were actually free. We were able to visit most all of Lyle's family, my son and daughter, and our two grandchildren.

On our way home we toured Pierre, South Dakota and the Black Hills. Lyle went down the water slide when we were at the hot springs located in Hot Springs, SD. Later, we walked through the woods and marveled at the huge rocks that look like giant petrified trees. We took the tour bus up to the lighting of the faces on Mount Rushmore. On the way home we drove through a very desolate part of Wyoming, and stopped at the Fort Phil Kearny battlefield near Buffalo, Wyoming. We were impressed with Story and Buffalo; our thoughts were that we would like to retire in that area. Dayton, Wyoming was another place that we really liked. Land was scarce there due to the large Padlock Ranch. It was established in 1943 and encompasses 475,000 acres that straddles the Montana and Wyoming state line Lyle's nephew, Bernard, and his wife, Becky had stopped over on their way to Washington. I rode with Becky and Bernard rode with Lyle as far as Billings. We went on to Red Lodge and over the hill to Belfry where we saw the memorial to the 72 miners who had lost their lives years ago. This trip was our reward for taking most of July to work on my office. We stayed at a nice campground on the way to Cody, and toured a bird sanctuary. Lyle took lots of pictures. We saw so many unusual and beautiful birds. There were also some angry and aggressive birds. An Emu tried to attack Lyle. It is a good thing the sanctuary was fenced. We toured the Big Horn visitors center and then came home via alternate highway 14, a 58-mile paved highway over the crest of the Big Horn Mountains. The pickup kept heating up but we made it to the top. We stopped at the Medicine Wheel again. Its history is a secret only the long-ago Native Americans know. The bighorns are truly Gods Paradise and we loved to spend time there. This trip we stayed at the Tie Flume campground.

Lyle went fishing and had a run in with a cow moose. He felt lucky to get back to the pickup alive. The cow had a calf and having Gunner along riled the moose up; she came after Lyle instead of the dog. All he had to defend himself with was a fishing pole. The moose would rear and come towards him then run back to her calf. Each time Lyle thought he was a goner. He was finally able to back most of the way up the hill and away from the moose. Some campers were nearby and offered him some water and a place to rest. When he finally got back to the camper, I asked him if he had caught any fish. He told me no fish and he'd been chased by a moose. I thought he was kidding. It was a long time before Lyle would even get near a moose even in the safety of the pickup. We went home after his run in with the moose and he came home as tired as he'd left.

Over Labor Day we went to Great Falls and toured the Charlie Russell Museum and the parks along the Missouri River as well as the dam. The museum was excellent and we enjoyed the sights; we even picked watercress out of the flowing spring in the park, and had that in our salad for supper. We weren't able to find a quiet campground so that trip turned out to be tiring.

Several years later we took Lyle's great great nephews (Steve's sons) to see these beautiful sites.

Our next trip was to Cooke City and Yellowstone Park to see how much damage the 1988 fires had done. We camped in a beautiful place on Rock Creek Friday, October 21st, then drove over Beartooth Pass the next day. The Beartooth Highway is U.S. Route 212 between Red Lodge and Cooke City, Montana. It traces a series of steep switchbacks to the 10,947 ft high Beartooth Pass. The highest part of the highway levels off into a wide plateau near the top of the pass then descends to where the Beartooth Highway connects to Wyoming Highway 296, the Chief Joseph Scenic Byway near Cooke City. This forms the northeast gateway to Yellowstone National Park.

On top of the Beartooth Spring of 2011

1988 cont:

This was the year Lyle decided to raise 200 chickens. By November 23 our freezer was full and we still had 40 roosters left to butcher. We decided that the next year we would let the one rooster we'd keep, and the hens, decide how many chickens we would raise. Definitely not 200!

Lyle tape recorded a loving message for me. I still have it; it is wonderful to hear his voice. It is especially treasured now that he is gone.

We finally quit smoking for good Thanksgiving of 1988. For Christmas I got Lyle the Victory At Sea video tapes. Lyle gave me a pretty sweat shirt and 3 beautiful scarf pins.

We went to the Jackpot for our 6th anniversary dinner. The sirloin steak wasn't that good. They had a country band; I was so disappointed because they didn't even know, "You Light Up My Life." When we went home, we went through our anniversary ritual, and I again shed happy tears because of Lyle's love for me.

1989:

Lyle's 53rd birthday was spent at home. We had that Chocolate Mallow Cake again. His gifts from me: A Franklin Speller, an Old Spice shaving mug, soap and brush, and a brass eye glasses holder. We went cross country skiing the next day, January 2nd.

Early February was so cold. It was 38 below in Colstrip. Lyle was a custodian at the elementary school in Colstrip. All the schools closed in Eastern Montana so he had a couple of days off. We stayed close by the fire. Lyle had harvested some Great Northern Beans from his garden so I made bean soup with ham.

Easter Sunday, we drove down to watch the ice jams on the Yellowstone River. Huge sections of ice, trees, and debris were jammed against the bridge. We walked on down to the dam and watched the ice tumble over it. It rained all night so that added to the flooding.

We had quite a snow storm in May. And the roof on the wonderful trailer I found started to leak! Lyle had to get up on the roof and shovel the snow off then repair it after it dried.

We spent 2 weeks in Wisconsin in June. In August I made one of the biggest mistakes of our life together. We bought 2 mares; one with a foal at side. Had we bought 2 saddle horses and stopped it would have been so much better. Raising horses took time away from Lyle even though he helped, and it added financial stress to our lives. He enjoyed riding and loved taking the horses to the Big Horns, and even to Yellowstone Park. We would have done that a lot more often but we had mares, foals, and stallions to care for. He looked forward to the foals but 2 saddle horses would have had us looking to the mountains a lot more often.

On our way to get the horses we stopped and camped in the Big Horns. Lyle lost his reading glasses and we never did find them.

It is a good thing we quit smoking the fall of '88 because Lyle had to have heart surgery October 16, 1989. He had 5 by-passes. Lyle would not have lived to have the surgery if we had continued smoking. Neither of us had will power so we had to quit at the same time. When his condition was diagnosed, I had been watching him out the window. He acted like he was so tired; just totally all in.

I made an appointment with our local doctor who sent him to a Cardiologist in Billings. His diagnosis was critical yet the doctor sent us home and scheduled his surgery in 2 days. We had no idea that doctor was from New Jersey and didn't realize how far we lived from Billlings; almost 100 miles one way. But by the Grace Of God Lyle lived to have the surgery. His heart served him well for 24 more years.

Lyle didn't go back to work until 2 days before Christmas. Lloyd's widow, Grace, and Rene were coming for a visit on Amtrak so we were going to pick them up in Glasgow. The day before it was down to 40 below. The propane wouldn't even flow. In the meantime, the water froze. We were out of everything but wood heat when we got home from work. Lyle built a fire under the propane tank and it did start flowing to the furnace and water heater.

When we returned from Glasgow the temperature was 40 above; chinook winds had blown in from the north. Rene went on to visit her girl friend for Christmas. Grace spent Christmas and our anniversary with us. Grace was with us for New Year's Eve and Lyle's birthday too.

My next regret started in 1990. I had this idea of a game that would help people understand recovery. That took so much time and money, and it was a bust. I even tried to market it at a chemical dependency seminar in California. As I was ready to leave for the seminar Lyle said, "No matter how this turns out remember that I love you and I'm here for you." It was a disaster and I was so depressed, and he was there for me! I think I mentioned that one of my characteristics was Eccentric, and that Lyle never had a dull moment but I felt a lot of sadness for the stress I caused him.

1990 was not a good year. We still had our ritual anniversary December 30th. We'd had arguments over that damn game so the year had not ended on a "happily ever after" note. Robin had been diagnosed with multiple sclerosis and had lost the sight in her right eye. Thankfully, we were able to help her financially.

1991: Lyle was 55 and he was depressed over his age. I gave him a Remington 243 and a box of shells. We had Chocolate Mallow Cake.

This was not the best year either; so much stress brought on by my "pig headedness". Remember Lyle's letter when he said I was "pig headed?" My self-esteem went south with the failure of the board game, and the horses were tiring both of us. Just too much with our jobs.

And to top it all off I felt as guilty as sin for what I'd been putting Lyle through but didn't know how to get out of the horses. I had given up on the game as it was a failed project.

That cost us a lot of money and it was very hard on our marriage. I didn't record our 9th anniversary although we went through our rituals; they didn't feel as good because of my actions. We spent Lyle's birthday driving to Havre so Rene could catch the train to Red Wing. She had been in Great Falls, and Havre was the closest Amtrak station. That trip was stressful and tiring.

OUR NEW HOUSE

1992: THE GOOD news for this year was our bid had been accepted on our home; a stick built home and not a trailer house. Did I ever wish I had the money I spent on that game to spend on remodeling this house? We did clean and paint. Lyle was so tired though because his job was not easy then to come home and work some more.

We remodeled the basement so I could move my office from town. It was a walk-in so met safety requirements. Keith and Dan came home and helped us move household belongings and a steel pole barn. The house had electric baseboard heat so we had a gas furnace installed. What a tiring year. I don't remember what we did for our Anniversary. I do know we played our wedding tape and went through our rituals, and again I was so thankful for my husband.

1993: I made the Chocolate Mallow Cake for Lyle's 57th birthday. We had gone through the Diet Center program a few years before this and lost a lot of weight. This was the last year for this cake because we were gaining weight again; after this it was Angel Food. The summer of '93 was more restful but Lyle fenced and fenced some more. He put a solid board fence all the way around our yard and built a deck and a better set of steps onto the house.

We painted the garage and house, and Lyle installed garage door openers. We even washed and sealed the garage floor. It looked sharp until the first rain when our dirt road was turned to mud.

We would park outside the garage but eventually gave up and just used a broom instead of mopping and sealing the floor. Lyle put the wood stove, from his house in Wisconsin, in the garage so he had heat and could work out there. He always had the radio on an old country music station.

When I thought I was in big trouble I had backed through the garage door. I couldn't believe how calmly Lyle responded to this; he was even nice about it. I was programmed from childhood to fear the reaction of the man in my life beginning with my step father. I was so afraid of being criticized, and worse yet told how dumb I was. Lyle never raised his voice and even hugged me. He wanted new garage doors anyway.

In July Rene and her husband came for a visit. We took a trip to Yellowtail Dam and the Big Horn Canyon. The trip up river was on a pontoon boat with a motor. A black bear was by the shore, and several deer were on the canyon hillside. We took this same trip with some friends years later.

We had gone to a friend's place in Miles City for Christmas dinner. Lyle wasn't feeling very good that day. 2 days later I got the flu and we were both sick. Our 11th Anniversary was spent going from the bed to the bathroom. Lyle got better before I did so he took care of me. When he promised to care for me, he meant it, and he never complained. I was the complainer! As Lyle would say, "You sound like a Fishmonger's wife ", however that was supposed to sound.

He did get me a beautiful card which we dated and kept just as we did with our cards and notes throughout all the years, we were together.

The 11 years had gone by so quickly. I had written in my journal that I would marry Lyle again except I'd certainly do so a lot sooner. We skipped our anniversary ritual though.

1994: No Chocolate Mallow Cake this birthday; Lyle's 58th. I had gotten him a coat; and my gift buying sorely lacks; it was too big and out of style. He was able to take it back and get what he wanted. I spent the first 2 weeks of January recovering from the flu.

We started remodeling the bathroom. The tub was set and Lyle had the plumbing installed. We even managed to paper an entire wall without arguing. Even when we did argue we usually couldn't even remember what it was about. Lyle was able to do so many things, and one of his attributes of many was, "He enjoyed the process of whatever he was doing!" My goal was to get it "done."

The Los Angeles earthquake happened while we were working on the bathroom. We were able to watch all the chaos on TV; imagine being able to see things as they occur. Neither of us had seen a TV until we were in our teens.

Gunner was getting gray around his muzzle and Fred was fatter and slept a lot. She and Gunner shared a blanket. Fred adored Lyle; she would sleep on his chest if he was lying down.

Lyle had a big garden again as usual, and he had planted trees, roses, and lilacs. His love of gardening extended into canning the produce. He enjoyed canning where I found it to be tedious work. I guess that comes from marrying at 16 and starting a wife and mother career long before I should have. By the time Lyle got me I was "burned out." He would tease me saying, "he got me too late."

The high point in '94 was Becky and her daughters' visit. We went to the Big Horn Mountains and drove up to the top of the canyon. Lyle, Becky, and the girls walked down the mountain. In places it was pretty treacherous; they had to cross the very swift Tongue River by jumping from rock to rock. We also took a canoe and float trip down the Yellowstone River.

In August Lyle and I went to Thermopolis, Wyoming. It is famous for its hot springs. Lyle especially enjoyed The Star Plunge, a privately operated water-park with a great water slide. A young man made the remark, "have at it, old man." That didn't stop Lyle from many trips down that water slide.

My diary keeping ended. We were working on the house plus our jobs and caring for the animals. We kept planting trees; so many that they started to shade the garden in later years.

We took a trip to Idaho for peaches. We bought 30 lugs as people had asked us to bring peaches back for them too. This paid for a special trip since we came home through Yellowstone Park. A buffalo was holding up traffic in the opposite lane. We thought that rather funny, but just around the corner a buffalo was in our lane, and he was not going to move faster than a slow walk.

BACK COUNTRY DRIVING

TAKING THE BACK roads with Lyle was not for the faint hearted. Even driving across the pasture didn't faze him but I was worried about big holes, rocks, and all the other things a person couldn't see. Didn't faze him; that is until we'd ran into it.

Snow drifts didn't bother him; they were a challenge and he "didn't even need 4-wheel drive."

Sometimes he made it and frequently he didn't. I think the reward was in the trying. When all else failed he either used 4-wheel drive or got stuck.

Lyle found icey roads a challenge also. If there was an icey, vacant area he loved to spin the car around. He said that he and his friends would drive out onto Lake Pepin after it froze solid.

They would drag race, dare each other, and spin their cars around. Fast driving was normal for them.

We took several trips to the Pryor Wild Horse Range. On one of those trips Lyle drove up a gravel creek. It wasn't very deep but I was a wreck. Then he tried for a steep, muddy road on a hillside. That did it; if he didn't turn around and get back to civilization I was going to walk.

The next time we set out to see the wild horses he took a different route. The road was steep and rough but dry. We saw lots of horse manure but no horses. Lyle thought we should be able to go across the mountain to Lodge Grass. We came to a place where the road was not to be challenged. He was going to try it. Again, I threatened to just get out and walk.

He reminded me so much of my grandfather. He would drive where angels would fear to tread.

Neither Lyle or my grandfather ever had a wreck but their situations were not for cowards.

As Lyle's health started to fail, he became more cautious. I guess the rough roads he liked to travel were similar to the rough spots on the road of life and marriage; journeying together over the rocky roads. I never did get out and walk; the threats worked. So, our road trips turned out okay and so did our marriage.

MORE EXPLORING

WE HAD GONE to a Sportsman Expo at the Metra in Billings. They had different prizes and we won a weekend in Cooke City. Our motel and meals were furnished along with a tank of gas.

After the weekend was up, we put our tent up and stayed a few more days. If I had read of all the bear and human altercations in that area, I'd have been too scared to camp in a tent. I guess ignorance is bliss or what you don't know won't hurt you.

We took advantage of a medical appointment Lyle had in Bozeman; his mileage was paid by the VA. We came home by way of Cooke City, and stayed at the Soda Butte Lodge. It was a very nice place to stay, and we enjoyed our meals in the Prospector Restaurant. When he had an appointment at the VA in Helena we went on to the Gates Of The Mountains, and took the tour boat up the Missouri River. Lyle loved Lewis and Clark history so this was a special day for him. Meriwether Lewis had written "In many places the rocks seem ready to tumble on us. At each bend in the waterway, great stone walls seemed to block passage, only to open like gentle giant gates as the expedition drew near." In his journal, Meriwether wrote: "I shall call this place: "GATES OF THE MOUNTAINS". The tour lasted 2 hours.

From the tour boat we could see Mann Gulch, site of the forest fire that killed 13 smoke jumpers over 50 years ago. There is a book about the fire and also a movie. Richard Widmark acted in "Red

Skies Over Montana ". The book by Norman Maclean is "Young Men and Fire".

We saw Osprey nests, eagles, vultures, and falcons. We were hoping to see bear or deer but they weren't to be seen. Grand scenery with wooded slopes and unique, rugged rock formations made for a wonderful trip. And the placid beauty of the Missouri, a river Lyle was fascinated by.

One of Lyle's favorite books was "Undaunted Courage", the story of Lewis and Clark by Hugh Ambrose. He also wrote another of Lyle's favorites, "Pacific" about World War II. Hugh Ambrose died in early June 2015 at the age of 48.

Lyle wasn't able to walk very far because of his back. He started having back problems in '94 and it never got any better. He was always in pain. He had several surgeries where the surgeon tried to free pinched nerves but those surgeries didn't help.

When we were talking about all the years he'd suffered with back and groin pain he blamed it on his job as a custodian, vacuuming class rooms 5 days a week with a vacuum that usually needed new brushes and belts. Lyle didn't care for his job but once he had heart surgery the school's insurance became critical, and he stayed even though it was difficult.

Lyle regretted his life choices. He wanted to re-up in the Navy but his parents were elderly and needed his help. He recalled asking his mother if they were actually making a living on the farm. She never answered him. His Dad would promise a pay check when the lambs were shipped, and when they were they couldn't afford to pay him. When Lyle looked back on his life, he wasn't happy about the sacrifices he had made. His Dad had made the same sacrifices by living on a farm next to his mother's place, and his farm was laid out on hills that weren't conducive to farming. Lyle said his mother had always resented that.

AGING AND LOSS

OUR LIFE TOGETHER was strengthened by friendship, but we did grieve for the youth and young love we had missed. That saying, "grow old with me the best is yet to come," is not true, but it would have been a lot worse if either of us had to go through those years alone.

Along with his health came very painful losses as his sisters, nephews Bernard, Art, Steven, and his niece, Wilma, passed away. They were more like siblings. Lyle was a change of life baby so he was closer in age to his nieces and nephews. They had spent their youth together running the hills on the farm, fishing, and hunting. Many hot days were enjoyed at their swimming hole on Rush River. To create some excitement in our life I decided we needed a couple of goats to eat weeds, so we got Sweetheart Darlin and Lisa. They were a pain from the start. When they kidded it was below zero, and the kids nearly froze to death, so we brought them into the house to warm up. We didn't have the goats very long when we returned them to the people, we bought them from. Remember, Lyle hated goats and these didn't try to endear themselves to him. He had tried to milk Sweetheart Darlin and she fought him every step of the way. That feeling of dislike was mutual, and they didn't eat weeds but loved roses.

We spent our anniversaries and Lyle's birthdays at home. The thought of coming out of a restaurant, or even going to one, in the cold weather didn't appeal to us. Being together was important and there was no place like home.

I had written in my journal that "I was thinking about my life, looking back into my childhood, wondering what my life would be like. Well, I am with the man I love, a once-in-a-lifetime true love. The negatives of my life are my daughter's multiple sclerosis, family deaths, Keith and Rene's diabetes, and the problems Lyle is having with his health. He is still my handsome husband and more than I ever dreamed of when I was a girl."

Lyle liked birds. He had feeders in the front and back yards, and he built blue bird houses that he hung on pasture fence posts. Finches, chats, robins, orioles, and jays were the birds that came to the feeders. We had one chickadee come to our feeder. The woods were too far from our place so anything we had to offer didn't attract them. My grandmother Poloson had so many chickadees every winter. She cooked for the birds and the dogs. One didn't run out and buy dog or bird feed in those days.

Our road drifted something awful when Lyle went to get the mail with the car. The road was drifted, the transmission went out, the car got stuck, and the diesel pickup quit. We had one of our worst arguments; both of us were hurt and angry and that carried into the next day. We made up a bit then started all over again. And the worst was I couldn't even remember why, and I don't think Lyle did either. After the transmission was fixed and it was 18 below Lyle got stuck again coming up the driveway with the car. Our arguments usually ended with neither of us recalling how it had started.

Lyle retired in 2001. He went out with a crash when he fell off the ladder in the garage, and cracked a couple of ribs, a few days before his retirement date. He had total knee replacement surgery right after his 65th birthday. We had a very quiet birthday celebration, and for our 19th anniversary December 30th we just exchanged cards. Multiple sclerosis had taken Robin's life February 19, 2006. She was 41 years old. We had made reservations for Yellowstone Park for that weekend, and were looking forward to a snow coach trip through the park. A deputy came to the house that evening and we canceled our trip immediately. We left for California in early March to visit Dan's family, Keith's family, and bring Robin's ashes home.

We buried her ashes in the Lonepine Cemetery June 24, 2006. Her suffering had ended.

The night Robin died I cried so much and Lyle felt helpless; how does one stop such pain? I am thankful he was with me. Going through that without him would have been so much worse. I know he felt the same way with the deaths of his sisters, niece, brother, and nephews. He was not alone.

"The pain of love is the pain of being alive. It is a perpetual wound. "This quote by Maureen Duffy, an English writer.

When Bob & Therese came to visit, they helped bring in the rest of the tomatoes. It was due to freeze any night. Lyle got out his slide projector and showed some slides from the 1960's. They also helped Lyle get some more wood cut. Bob was practicing with the Bobcat skid steer. The Beartooth Mountains had 10 inches of snow, and a cold wind had blown all day, but it didn't freeze in the low lands.

We all drove to the Big Horn Mountains and enjoyed a picnic at the Tongue River trail head by Dayton, Wyoming. That afternoon we went on up to Bear Lodge. It was hunting season so not an animal anywhere. We did see a lone coyote along the highway in the Rosebud Valley. He was still there when we came back; must have been some good mousing in that area.

Lyle had 2 favorite sayings: "I don't suffer fools" and "No good deed goes unpunished."

He read Stephen King books. Scary stories didn't bother him, and the same for scary movies. I didn't like scary or violent. He said we were going to see "Gandhi ". He assured me there wouldn't be any violence because Gandhi was not a violent man. What he didn't tell me was the fact that Gandhi suffered through a lot of violence, and was murdered. The next movie was "Silence Of The Lambs." When I saw lambs in the title, I thought the movie would have something to do with farming or ranching. When the extreme violence began it was all I could do to set through the movie. Lyle thought that was so funny. Like I said, "He married me so he'd have someone to laugh at."

Mom had major surgery at Mayo (St Mary's Hospital) October of 2007. My sister and I stayed in Rochester for a week. Mom came to our place that December so she'd have care during her recovery. She had Christmas, our anniversary, and Lyle's birthday with us. Mom left for her daughter's March 16th then on to Red Wing April 1, 2008. She passed away December 20, 2008. Winter storms prevented us from traveling to her funeral in Red Wing. We did have a memorial at Lonepine in July of 2009.

Therese had an audit in the Billings area right after the 2008 Christmas so she drove to our place to visit, and went with us for our anniversary dinner. She drove through some awful weather on her way back to Billings. Lyle got a card from me and no cake for his birthday.

Lyle had total shoulder replacement January 29, 2009. He developed blood clots after the surgery so was in critical care. He was committed to the painful rehab process after he came home, his new shoulder never gave him problems.

He was able to build the hay barn and put up a greenhouse then build a new deck by the back door. He planted and cared for a big garden, built raised beds in his greenhouse and garden, and cut up winter fire wood. We had bought a Maytag refrigerator at Lowes with a $150 cash rebate. When we went to Billings, he used that to buy the PVC decorative rails for the back deck and steps.

My workaholism is and was a curse. Internet horse sales had me way too busy. I developed the Part Walking Horse Registry in 1999. We sold that to a company in California in 2008. I retired totally from selling horses over the internet October 31, 2008. I finally had more time for Lyle, myself, reading, and home.

2011: Son Of The Morning Star aka "Herman" had to be put down due to chronic laminitis. Lyle cried for days over his death. He'd spent so much time with him from the hour he was foaled, and he'd ridden him in the hills. Herman had a way about him that almost made a person think he could communicate. He was our granddaughter's guy too; when she was a little girl, she said she wanted to marry Herman. She could ride him all over the pasture without a bridle, halter, or saddle. He'd even get close to the fence or trailer so it was easier for her to get on.

2011 was the year we got rid of all of the horses except Fawn and Marigold. We still had the chickens, and Lyle and a friend bought 50 fryers; they fattened these and we all shared in butchering and divided the meat. With the price of feed and all the extra work we could have bought Hutterite chickens, and came out ahead. Butchering chickens wasn't my favorite job.

We had the upstairs and downstairs bathrooms tiled, and installed a whirlpool bath. That tub was heavy but Lyle and I managed to get it into the basement room where he could hook it up to water and a drain. He had already put the drain and plumbing in before the tub arrived. When he remodeled for my office, he had built a bathroom, and installed a toilet and sink.

If I even mentioned having some of that work done by someone else Lyle would not hear of it!

He maintained the car and pickups, the Ford 8N, the skid steer, lawnmowers, and sprayed for weeds and mosquitoes. Not long before he died, we needed a new kitchen faucet. I was going to call a plumber but he said he could do it, but he did let me help. We had to use the sawzall to free the old faucet. Lyle would rest then work on it some more. He finally got it done.

LYLE'S LIFE IN PICTURES

LYLE BROUGHT A bouquet of red roses in for me. They were beautiful and lasted quite a while after they were cut. The roses below are William Baffin. They are extra hardy.

I took this picture in April of 2014. Lyle planted all the roses, trees, and shrubs on our place. There wasn't a tree or bush on our place when we moved there in '92.

Lyle had been picking apples by the 5-gallon bucket full. Some from our trees and more from the neighbor's trees. He canned 50 qts. of applesauce and froze apple slices for crisps and pies. We had bought a dehydrator so we dried lots of apples too. I made a lot of apple crisps.

Lyle greenhouse and antique corn planter

Lyle's Giant Sunflower

His Linden Tree (pride and joy)

Once In A Lifetime Comes A Man

Lyle and Grace Fawn and Son Of The Morning Star (Herman) Black Hills 2007

Lyle & Fawn (his cavalry hat)

Lyle and Orphan filly, Boo 1999

Lyle started the outdoor furnace October 11, 2013

2013; the last winter Lyle had at our place

We had firewood brought in from 2011 on. Lyle would saw it up then split it with the wood splitter.

When we were young in the late '90's we had cut some good-sized trees down in the Custer Forest. Lyle cut them into 12 foot lengths so they'd fit on the flatbed trailer. We rolled every one of those onto that trailer.

Another time we had a semi load of baled hay brought in. There were over 600 - 80 lb bales and we stacked every one of them by hand. We were soft when we started and in great shape when we finished.

MORE TRIPS, FAMILY, AND WOOD

LYLE'S RETIREMENT WOULD have been so much nicer if he hadn't been in pain so much of the time. We did take more trips. Once to the Grand Canyon and at least 3 trips to Yosemite. We went to Sea World and the San Diego Zoo during our trip to San Diego, and ate at places where the food was exceptional. Keith and his wife treated us and even paid for our trip.

We took a trip to Jackson Hole then went into Idaho. We spent time camping in Glacier Park. Another time we went to Oregon, and far enough into California to see the big trees.

Lyle asked me to read the map and find a campground. Since I had seldom ever had need for a map, I was clueless on how to find camp sites. I told him there were campgrounds all along the highway we were traveling on. When he finally stopped the pickup and read the map, Oh, Oh!

I was in big trouble. He was tired and so was I. We had Gunner with us too. He wanted to see the sand dunes so we stopped and walked about. Lyle had bought some chicken at a drive in; he asked me if I wanted any but I was pouting, so no chicken for me. As we walked the sand dunes Lyle had his chicken in his hand, and his arm was at his side. Gunner came along and grabbed the chicken. Since I was pouting, I thought that served Lyle right.

The one time after we left Yosemite, we went on to see the big Sequoia trees. Lyle loved the ocean and always wanted to go back one more time. We had a nice trip to the Flathead in March of 2010. That year we had a perfect trip to Minnesota and Wisconsin to visit family. Other trips took us to the Black Hills and our beloved Big Horns.

When our granddaughter, Amber, spent summers with us she went on camping and trail riding trips to the Big Horns. Over the years, we took many trips to the Big Horn Battlefield. Lyle was able to meet his family at the Theodore Roosevelt Park in North Dakota several years before he died. He enjoyed his great great nieces, and nephew. Lyle lived to see and know all eight of these children. Their Grandpa, Bernard, had died before they were born so Lyle became their Papa.

Steve and Patty's sons, Jake, Luke, and Zach spent several vacations at our place. Lyle took them to Thermopolis. They spent time camping, horseback riding, and helping Lyle. Rachel didn't care for the guy things, but Lyle looked forward to his visits with her too. He loved all his nieces, nephews, great nieces and nephews, and great-great nieces and nephews. They were the light of his life. He looked forward to their cards and phone calls.

When Lyle and the boys went to Thermopolis, they set their tent up then went swimming. When they returned the wind had blown the tent into the water faucet, turned it on, and the tent was soaked. Calls from his sisters were special. He and Shirley would remember and recite poems and share memories. Violet said Lyle was her baby; she was 13 when he was born and delighted in helping their mother care for him.

When I went to my mother's funeral in 2009 Bob and Therese stayed with Lyle and helped with the yard and chores. Lyle was in so much pain that summer. They helped finish our roof during a visit in 2007. Lyle had half of it finished when they came. He was 71 years old and still able to get up on the roof and handle 16-foot sheets of steel. Lyle always had excellent flexibility; he could still touch his toes the year he died.

Kenny and Lori had been able to come visit after they were married. Kenny helped Lyle build a big feed bin for the barn. Art and Opal came to visit several times over the years and Lyle was able to visit with Art a few months before he passed away. When I took a trip to California Becky came out and stayed with Lyle so he wouldn't be alone. They went to Thermopolis and enjoyed the hot springs. His nephew, Allen and friend, Lamoine, made the trip from Colorado Springs to our place a few years before Lyle passed away. He had a great time with them, a visit that also took in the Black Hills.

My sons had come home several times over the years to help out. They helped us move and rebuild the barn in '92. Keith did all the duct work for our furnace. Lyle got a laugh out of being called a Peon; he was Keith's assistant.

The last load of fire wood Lyle cut. He cut this and more in less than 20 minutes. He was a skilled chain saw man, and it would take a heck of a man to surpass him even in his last days.

This was taken 16 days before his death. He had to take oxygen everywhere he went the last months of his life. Our best times were cutting wood whether at home or in the forest. We prized the days we spent together gathering fire wood. We were quite a team, as Lyle used to say.

Lyle was usually a very patient man. The two things that brought out his impatient side were going after wood, and driving with a lost back seat driver. Actually, any back seat driver.

Lyle could also back seat drive but that didn't count. Usually, it was easier to let him drive than to have him "directing" my driving. I seemed to be able to hit every pot hole when he was with me!

Going after wood was fun after we were going down the road. Lyle would be in such a hurry to get going. "Wasn't I ready yet? What was taking me so long?" What he forgot was what he needed to get ready for the woods.

We had gone to the Custer Forest about 90 miles from home. When we got there, he became aware he had forgotten chain saw oil. So, we went bumping off across country to a little store in Sonnette. Luckily, they had oil.

Another time I asked him to stop for the trailer spare tire; he had driven right by it. "No time for that", he was in a hurry. We had rolled those big logs on the trailer so it was heavily loaded.

We were almost to Colstrip when a tire went flat. Lyle limped the trailer in to town and parked it in an empty lot. I did say I told you so and also that I was not going with him the next day when he went after it.

Usually, he had the patience of Job. I never did figure out what it was about these situations, and there were many, that caused him to wear blinders. He focused so much on getting me ready to go, or telling me how to drive. If I was driving that really tried his patience.

Even though these situations were stressful at the moment they were also funny afterwards.

OUR LOVE NOTES

Our First Anniversary (June 1983)

Yesterday was our anniversary, a remembrance of
the day of our lives intertwined and began
Oh, how I anticipated our meeting on that
beautiful June evening
Butterflies raced through my being
While my heart beat with wild abandon
I was to be with you again, something
I'd thought just a dream for so long

As my moment of arrival neared, I really
began to believe seeing you was for real
As I drove the miles to your home
the landscape was changed so much by nature
that I couldn't remember the countryside
Was I lost or almost there?

I stopped and ask the neighbor
then raced my car onward to your door
You are not at home so disappointed yet
relieved, I drove on
What would you think of me now?
It has been so long since you saw me

Once In A Lifetime Comes A Man

I drive on up the road to your brother's
my heart is in my hands
I walk shakily to their doorstep
They welcome me and make me feel at home

The phone rings and it is you
Am I there yet?
Again my heart races with wild abandon
I can't wait to be by your side

Soon we are greeting each other
both nervous and scared
The years have been good to you I think
as I drink of your handsome profile
and listen to the music of your voice

I fear that you will not see
the girl from long ago but
you saw her and much more
and here we are together this June
savoring memories of that special
summer evening one year ago

To my husband, Lyle, with all my love

and gratitude for loving me, for giving my
life meaning and joy, and for sharing all
of the good and bad. I love you more today
than I did yesterday, and I will love you more
tomorrow.
With Love, Grace

Some of our Anniversary Notes

Twenty Years

With Love & Thankfulness For
Each Day With You. The Twenty
Years We Have Shared Have
Been The Best Years Of My Life!
I Love You And Cherish Your Love
For Me.

With Love, Grace Poohduk

Twenty Ninth Year

On our life's journey,
we've celebrated the peaks,
passed through a valley or two,
and you've always been
right by my side

Looking back, I'm amazed and grateful
for every step we've taken together
and I can't wait to see
where tomorrow brings us
With Lots Of Love Grace DUK

For My Wife
With All My Love
"All the words in the world
can't even start
to tell of the love
that's in my heart"
To the greatest, Love Lyle
One of my last cards to Lyle

On the back of the card: "I have never stopped
thanking God for you" Ephesians 1:16
I had written on the inside "I love you
more than words can say" DUK

Notes And Plaques From Lyle

Plaque: "I love you more today than yesterday, and only half as much as tomorrow."

Plaque: "Love is eternal like the circle of a ring, whole unto itself, it's beauty ending but going on forever."

Notes: "Welcome home Dear, sorry about what Fred did to your office."

"I really, really missed you." Love XXXXX Lyle "The machine is fixed. I love you hugely."

"The sheets are washed and the bed made. Welcome home, Darling."

"Duk, on our second Christmas. Wishing it was our twenty second." Your Loving Lyle.

December 30, 1999

Dearest Lyle,
I am very grateful for your love, and the fact that you still love me after putting up with my idiosyncrosies for 17 years!
I LOVE:
1. Your wonderful memory & all the knowledge you have and share with me and others.
2. That you go to a job you don't like every day to support us.
3. You are Handsome & Smart!
4. My Heart still does its flips over you!
5. Your love for our horses and the new foals.
6. Your support no matter what.
7. The loving patience that you have as you care for me when I am hurt or sick.
8. The friendship I have with you.
9. The relationship you have with your special nieces & nephews.
10. Your love and concern for Robin and Rene.
11. Your love for Dan, Keith, and Kevin; with Kevin even though he has never given you any reason to care for him.
12. Your voice over the phone is PERFECT.
13. The way you looked for me when I took Misty to the other pasture. You were concerned.
14. The bright white ceiling you put in the office and the store room.
15. All the basement window covers.
16. All the fencing and water systems.
17. All the trees, shrubs, and flowers, and the nice garden with luscious vegetables.
18. All the mechanical on the cars and pickups.
19. All the stalls in the barn along with the tack storage cupboards, saddle racks, bridle & halter hangers, etc.
20. The fun we shared on the trail rides or just riding close to home.
21. I admire the way you ride and how you handle your horse so gently.
22. That you fix breakfast most of the time and help with other meals.
23. That you shampoo our carpets and help with the major cleaning.
24. Your love for animals and birds and the environment.
25. That you are down to earth and realistic about our earth and world affairs.
26. I am never bored being with you.
27. I am excited each time you come in the door from work, town, or just being outside.
28. The fact that Holidays are not a big thing for you and that you respect my beliefs.
29. For building the very nice Decks onto our house; the back deck makes it so much easier to take clothes to the line.
30. For all of the things you say & do that I haven't listed on here.
31. I would be lost without you!!
32. And most of all I love you just BECAUSE!!

With all of my Love,
Duk

Valentine's Day 1985

My Darling Husband,

Today I love you and appreciate all of your qualities even more than I did yesterday, and I thought I loved you as much as possible. Each day I find more reasons to be thankful for your love & companionship. I became so emotional when 20-20 was on because they played Endless Love, and a couple who have had 70 years of marriage said they used Ruth's Story, in song,"Whither Thou Goest I Will Go." I thanked God for you and my tears were of happiness.

Every minute of my day has meaning because I have your love. I have become more aware of life, pain, joy, and beauty because of your love. I have many reasons for living because you are here to share each day with me. I feel happy, confident, and enthusiastic because of you. I am seldom ever sad and sadness doesn't last because of you.

I am proud of you. I admire you. I need you. I trust you. And the way you think about problems in our families & then come up with sensible ideas always amazes me!

Thank you for loving me, Lyle.

Grace
DuK

Lyle & I 1985

Lyle & I 1994

OUR LAST DECEMBER

LYLE SAID HE'D never go anywhere carrying oxygen but eventually he did. He had a home oxygen concentrator but when we went anywhere, he had the portable tanks. He was diagnosed with Sleep Apnea and he never did get used to the required sleep apparatus.

Type 2 Diabetes was a significant health problem. He had so many bouts with low blood sugar.

It was especially difficult for me to recognize this when he was driving. He hated a "back seat driver" so if I said anything he had a strong reaction. This was a normal behavior so when the same happened with a blood sugar low I didn't recognize it at all.

The last episode with low blood sugar was the Wednesday before he died. We had gone to the store 7 miles from home. On the way back he insisted on driving down the center of the road. No cars were coming but I said something about his driving and he reacted. I was that so called fish monger's wife, and I don't even remember what I said he was. We arrived at the place and I asked him to back in; it would be easier to unload groceries. He started backing and kept backing right into the PVC fence. I was hollering and waving my arms. He ignored me and kept right on backing, this time into the garage. When he stopped, he had the back of the pickup against his table saw. Another 4 inches and he'd have pushed it out the back wall. I was really upset because he hadn't listened at all. This carried into the house. He said he thought I wanted him to back into the garage.

After he had some orange juice his mind cleared. He said to me, "Let's not spend our last days like this." That set me back into some humility, and I finally realized he'd had low blood sugar. How did he know his time was close? His hands were always cold and he said he didn't even have the strength to put the dishes away out of the dishwasher. These were all signs his health was getting much worse. I had asked him to go to the doctor the Friday before he died.

I was disappointed when he didn't see the younger doctor. I should have gone into the doctor's exam room with him. Lyle was retaining fluid and this doctor didn't take any extra measures. Whether a difference could have been made I will never know.

2 days before he died, he helped me with cleaning knick knacks that were up high along the kitchen walls. I would hand the items to him. After I washed them, he handed them back to me, and I put them up on their shelves. I gave him a big hug and he gave me one of his fabulous kisses that sent thrills clear down to my toes again. That was our last kiss! All through the years we had said, "I Love You", when we went to bed. We missed a few nights but very few.

Sunday, the 15th of December, was a good day. Lyle was in good spirits. I fixed porcupine meat balls, mashed potatoes, and green beans for supper. We had company and in our conversations our anniversary came up. We discussed plans and how going out for dinner would depend on the weather. We had decided that we'd better go through all of our anniversary rituals; we weren't getting any younger. Play our songs, light our candle, repeat our vows, and make it an evening to remember. Besides cold weather we were trying to think of a restaurant that served great food. We hadn't come to any decisions when we went to bed except if it was cold, we were staying home.

We visited for a while then I went to bed. I heard Lyle call, "Grace." He had fallen on his way to the bathroom. I helped him up and into the shower. He had problems stepping out of the shower but made it. I had a hold of him all the time so he wouldn't fall again. We walked into the bedroom and he laid down. I asked him if he wanted a cover and he said, "No." I sat down and had a cup of coffee. It was 3 AM and I am an early riser so there was no use of me going back to bed. I didn't hear Lyle get up but heard him fall. I was in the bathroom in seconds. He was already gone! I never looked at his face as I wanted to remember the first time ever, I had seen his face, and all the wonderful years afterwards. I called 911 and the neighbors. I was in shock.

Our neighbors came immediately. They were Lyle's adopted kids as we'd lived by them for so many years. Marsha made phone calls to Lyle's family. I wasn't emotionally strong enough to tell them their beloved brother and uncle was dead.

The weather was not good. We had a lot of snow, and it was cold. Becky called and said she and Bernie were coming. I told her they didn't need to make the trip in that weather. They came anyway and Bernie drove through some treacherous storms.

I had to wait until Tuesday (he had died early on Monday, the 16th) to make arrangements for his cremation and funeral. Those hours went by so slow. Once the funeral arrangements were made it seemed like "months" before Becky & Bernie arrived. I was so glad to see them.

Bernie drove during the time he was at our place; I wasn't in the real world yet. Bernie was so special to Lyle.

Becky helped me with the chores the morning of Lyle's funeral. The sky had been cloudy with no sign of blue. As we walked to the barn, we could see an opening and the sun coming through the clouds. A softness had come over the land, a special sight Lyle had always loved. On the way to town a lone eagle was in the field. The only time we'd ever seen eagles there had been several years before. A military service was planned. His funeral featured guards of honor and the firing of volley shots as a salute. He was cremated so the flag was given to me; otherwise, it would have been draped over his coffin.

I picked out a beautiful urn and an urn vault. The funeral director put all the photos I had taken in on photo boards, and kept the best for a DVD to show during his funeral. The songs were those Lyle had said he wanted except for Russ's Song. I chose that and even wore my wedding dress. Lyle's songs were Garden Party and The Last Thing On My Mind. Video music: How Great Thou Art, Eternal Father (Navy Hymn), and Paloma Blanca, also songs Lyle wanted. Chaplin Major Art McCaffrey officiated.

Stopping By The Woods On A Snowy Evening by Robert Frost, and the 121st Psalm were on his memorial brochure. A copy of the words to Russ's song was placed in each for the guests at his funeral.

When we discussed our last wishes, Lyle didn't want a memorial in Wisconsin because his loved ones would cry! We had one anyway on May 4, 2014. It was held at the American Legion Hall near

Maiden Rock, WI. That memorial was necessary so his loved ones and friends could say good-bye, and have some closure. Becky flew out to our place to help me pack for his memorial. We also packed keepsakes for his loved ones.

Becky helped me drive home then flew back to Wisconsin. We had a fun trip visiting places Bernard and Lyle had been to. One of those, Lemmon, SD is home to the world's largest Petrified Wood Park. This fills an entire block and is built entirely of petrified wood, fossils, and stone. There is a wishing well, a waterfall, a jail, and a castle. The castle weighs 300 tons and boasts towering spires and turrets. Also in the park are two separate museums, both built entirely of petrified wood. From there we drove through the Spearfish Canyon; so much beauty.

It is a good thing Becky was with me at our place. I had gone to feed the horses when the mare we were boarding kicked me in the face! Thank God for Bernie and Becky, and also Justin and Marsha. The stitching process hurt and novacain tastes terrible but the doctor did a fine job of stitching my upper lip inside and out, and I lived to talk about it!

Lyle's Hal at his Wisconsin Memorial

Display at Lyle's Wisconsin Memorial

Kenny and Grace holding Lyle's urn. Photo taken at his old Wisconsin farm

May 4, 2014. Kenny, Lyle's nephew, passed away August 30, 2014

Photo of our Urn Vault. I have Lyle's urn on the coffee table. When I die both of our urns will go into this vault, and be buried on our lot at the Murray Memorial Cemetery located at Lonepine, Montana

Lyle chose these words from his favorite Psalm 121. We had this grave stone made several years before Lyle's death.

MOVING ON

I MADE THE DECISION to sell our place near Forsyth the summer of 2014. I paid for Fawn's care after I moved to Kalispell. When the mare we had been boarding left I bought 2 wether goats to stay with Fawn in the pasture. They went back to the man I had bought them from after Fawn died. A lady came and got the hens, and a friend found a home for Charlie Cat with a family in Forsyth. Marigold died in 2012 and Fawn died in April of 2015. I had my special Millie kitty put to sleep. She was 14 and whenever I was gone, she would meow and could not be consoled. I can't have animals where I moved to, and she would not have moved comfortably. It would have been so stressful for her. I cried a lot until I finally made the decision. She was a 1-person kitty.

Charlie was Lyle's cat; he was a beautiful, big, yellow and white neutered male. Charlie would stand on end, sit, lay belly up, and anything else he could think of to make Lyle laugh.

Molly, our female Lab, moved next door. She spent some nights there anyway so her move wasn't traumatic.

The main reason for selling the place is I am accident prone. Most of my health problems have been caused by accidents since I was a young girl.

But, the sight of roses creates nostalgia and a sense of great loss. The loss of the Love Of My Life; My Brown Eyed Handsome Man.

On Memorial Day 2015 the Christmas Cactus I had bought for Lyle's funeral had one beautiful bloom.

Once In A Lifetime Comes A Man

The poem by Olive, below, and the next page entitled "Your A Sea Bee, You Can Take It" are dedicated to the memory of my Sea Bee, Lyle (Bud) Vernon Larson.

When Lyle was home on leave Olive had written a poem for him:

>A young lad and farmer named Lyle
>Has stayed with us for a while
>He has returned from the Navy
>Where all is not gravy
>And we love his tattoo and his smile
>Thanks for the cigarette
>Olive

"Your A Sea Bee, You Can Take It"

When you get up in the morning and look at your face,
Do you think it's a terrible disgrace?
Then out to master with that extra big head,
It really makes you wish you were dead.

You crawl on the manhaul and head for chow,
And every morning it's hotcakes somehow.
Then it's up to the job site and work half a day,
Come back at noon with even less pay.

Jump from the manhaul and run for the line,
If you think your first, you're out of your mind.
Once you're inside your troubles are through,
Cause they've got trays full of rice for you.

Here you're going back to work at noon,
And hoping the day is over soon.
Start shoveling gravel, And mixing mud,
Just another job for a crazy stud.

Filled the bucket and drop the load,
It means more points for the great big TOAD. (Officer in charge)
As we pour the last bucket into the wall,
Wouldn't you know it the rain did fall.

Back to the galley for fish heads an rice,

A T-bone steak would sure make it nice.
To B.P.H. as we proceed, (barracks post meal)
Along the way we light up of weed.

Dash from the hut and into the shower,
Cause liberty run leaves in an hour.
You hop in your civies and ready to go,
Come to find out you're too darn slow.

Arriving the village a little late,
So after all what's a date.
Sit on a bar stool and drink your fill,
Then the next morning what bar bill, Bill.

After a hard days work,
And a little nite fun,
What do you get????
ANOTHER, "WELL DONE"!!!!!

END PHOTOS

Sunset near our home

Shepherds Butte one of Lyle's favorite landmarks. It could be seen from our home.

Fall 1992 We had moved into our stick built home in May of 1992

Once In A Lifetime Comes A Man

Lyle 1966

Charlie

EPILOGUE

A PERSON'S LIFE IS a diary in which they plan to write one story but the unforeseen causes one to write another. In my humblest hour I compare the volume of our life as it was with what I had vowed to make it!

If I could relive and rewrite our life, I would forsake the workaholism and perfectionism, and my obsession with having a clean house; that had priority over all of our adventures. I would spend every possible minute with My Brown Eyed Handsome Man. Lyle's words of long ago: "I want to help you through life and beyond if it is possible. "He kept this vow clear to his death and beyond. It is profound that I was lucky enough to be his wife. I only hope I brought blessings to his life.

Throughout our years together I always marveled at Lyle's remarkable mind. His memory was like an encyclopedia with knowledge covering history, science, astronomy, the Bible, trees, plants, animals, and birds. He loved poetry and shared this love with his sisters. His love of reading was a gift from his mother and sisters. He built exceptional fences and buildings. And he also built beautiful book shelves, cabinets, and picture frames. I admired him so much because no matter what he was doing he was patiently involved in the process.

The love that he gave to me rarely comes along in anyone's lifetime. During our last days to-gether our love was deeper than life itself. Two people caring for one another as their time to-gether was getting shorter. Thank God for my wonderful husband. "Once In A Lifetime Comes A Man."

AUTHOR BIOGRAPHY

GRACE BAKER LARSON was born in Hot Springs, Montana in 1940. Her delivery was by a midwife. She grew up on a large sheep ranch that her grandparents owned. Her parents had divorced when she was eight months old. Grace describes herself as a jack of all trades and a master of none. She raised three sons and two daughters. Her daughter, Robin, died from MS when she was forty- one years old. Grace's husband passed away in December of 2013. Her life was controlled by circumstance until she and Lyle married. He was always there for her after that.

Grace has trained and shod horses, skidded logs, operated a day care center, cleaned houses, and spent fourteen years as a chemical dependency counselor. She was a journeyman painter for fourteen years. High work, spray painting, sandblasting, etc., for herself, contractors, and the Anaconda Company. She was the first woman to work in the trades in Anaconda Company History. She also worked as the inmate paint crew supervisor at the Montana State Prison.

Like Eleanor Roosevelt said, "You must do the thing you cannot do." Courage is fear that has said its prayers and that is how Grace made it through life until she married Lyle.

My son, Dan, passed away July 21, 2019. He was 53 years old.

www.ingramcontent.com/pod-product-compliance
Lightning Source LLC
Chambersburg PA
CBHW030152100526
44592CB00009B/237